LES ROUTIERS COOKBOOK

PAUL

FORRESTAL

LES ROUTIERS COOKBOOK

Foreword by
Raymond Blanc

EBURY PRESS · LONDON

First published by Ebury Press
an imprint of The Random Century Group
Random Century House
20 Vauxhall Bridge Road
London SW1V 2SA

British Library Cataloguing in Publication Data
Les Routiers cookbook : over 200 recipes selected by
Raymond Blanc.
1. Food – Recipes
I. Blanc, Raymond
641.5

ISBN 0–85223–951–3

Recipes compiled and tested by Jenny Horsley
Editor: Helen Southall
Designer: Bob Vickers
Photographer: Tim Hill
Stylist: Zoë Hill
Home Economist: Meg Jansz
Illustrations: Angela Barnes
Cover illustration: Bob Parker

Typeset in Linotron Palatino from disk by Textype Typesetters, Cambridge
Printed and bound in Great Britain by The Bath Press, Avon

CONTENTS

USING THE RECIPES IN THIS BOOK

* Use only one set of measurements, because imperial and metric are not exact equivalents.
* All spoon measures are level.
* All eggs used are size 3 unless otherwise stated.
* Use freshly ground rock salt and black pepper when seasoning is listed as an ingredient.
* Dry white wine has been used whenever white wine is listed unless otherwise stated.
* Use unsalted butter whenever possible.
* Use plain flour unless otherwise stated.
* Use fresh ingredients where possible.
* Use olive oil when oil is listed as an ingredient.

Foreword

Ever since my childhood in France I have regarded the red and blue Les Routiers symbol as a guarantee of quality and good value.

The emblem swung outside the local restaurant in our village of Saôme, attracting custom from passing travellers who knew they could expect a home-produced, unpretentious meal, bursting with flavour from fresh ingredients prepared by M. Michel, the *patron*. His 'vin de table' was drinkable by the jugful and diners found his cheerful company often encouraged them to linger for several hours over a coffee cognac, digesting his fare and conversation!

I vividly remember my first crossing of the Channel in 1972; I was served by a drunken English waiter who did not care about the amount of vinegar in the overcooked cabbage, nor the soggy chips, nor the way in which he displayed his bad manners – he also seemed to act with a very clear conscience. I knew that my trip across that tiny strip of sea was taking me to a world that was very different from the one that I had always known. This knowledge was subsequently highlighted at one of my first stops in a motorway café and restaurant; mediocrity, apathy, ignorance and lack of care appeared to be the main ingredients of the British catering industry. It was an industry affected by standardisation and an uninspired workforce led by conceited management forces who thought they knew better, but did not. Yet the customers seemed relatively pleased by the quality, or lack of it, as long as the ambience was right!

All this is part of the nightmare of yesterday. No longer could anybody say that you have to eat three breakfasts a day in England in order to eat well; this would smack of ignorance. For a country which is deeply rooted in tradition, change is normally painstakingly slow and yet so much has changed in Britain in the last fifteen years. Attitude, quality of service, understanding towards food and the rediscovery of adventure have all contributed to radical improvements.

However, much is still to be done. It is not difficult to find expensive restaurants whether they are good or bad, but we still badly lack the middle-priced good hotel or restaurant with simple hearty food.

Les Routiers have helped enormously to encourage, recognise and reward the small hotels and restaurants which have upgraded their standards. Indeed, in many cases, it has been the smaller independent restaurants (who form the bulk of Les Routiers members) that have led the trend towards setting better standards across the UK.

The famous red and blue sign sums up so much of the spirit of good French hospitality to me that when I opened my first restaurant in Britain – the Quat' Saisons in Oxford – I applied for one of the first British Les Routiers memberships. It wasn't just the symbol to hang on the wall either – we had to live up to a quality of lifestyle and eating the day it arrived, carrying on the tradition of the French roadside eateries. The immediate success and popularity of the restaurant allowed us to be rewarded the first year by the Routiers sign, but not the casserole (the Routiers symbol of excellence) mind you!

Now at Le Manoir I present a slightly different style of food, but the ingredients are still fresh, the wine still flows and our customers leave having experienced good value and warm hospitality, even if it is provided at a cost outside the Les Routiers price criteria!

The following recipe collection is made up of many of the most popular dishes served by the 1,800 UK Les Routiers members in their restaurants. Some are traditional ideas given an individual edge by the contributing member, others are innovative and fun, but all have been adapted and tested for easy preparation in the domestic kitchen.

I hope that you enjoy using this book to re-create some of the essence and atmosphere that is 'Les Routiers'; the art of good living, in your own home!

Raymond Blanc
Le Manoir aux Quat' Saisons
Great Milton
Oxfordshire

Summer 1990

BRUNCH

VERNA'S HOME-MADE MUESLI

WOODLAND DELL HOTEL
Lynton, Devon

Verna & Malcolm Holt

.

A fresh nutty muesli mix which can be stored in an airtight jar until required. Just before eating, sweeten with honey or dark brown sugar and serve with milk, cream or yogurt.

Serves 4–6

150 g (6 oz) oat flakes, or mixed oat flakes and bran
25 g (1 oz) hazelnuts, chopped
25 g (1 oz) almonds, chopped
25 g (1 oz) walnuts, chopped
25 g (1 oz) dried figs, chopped
25 g (1 oz) dried apricots, chopped
25 g (1 oz) sultanas
25 g (1 oz) raisins

1. Mix all the ingredients together in a large bowl. Serve at once or store in an airtight container until required.

PARKMOUNT PORRIDGE

PARKMOUNT HOUSE HOTEL
Forres, Moray

Angie & David Steer

.

Traditional Scottish porridge enriched with a sprinkling of whisky.

Serves 4

500 ml (1 pint) water
500 ml (1 pint) milk
125 g (5 oz) porridge oats
pinch of salt
30 ml (2 tbsp) whisky
30 ml (2 tbsp) dark brown sugar
either 50 g (2 oz) butter
or 125 ml (5 fl oz) double cream

1.   Cook the porridge according to the manufacturer's instructions or in the following traditional manner. Bring the water and milk to the boil in a pan. Pour in the oats in a steady stream, stirring them into the liquid. As soon as the mixture comes back to the boil, reduce the heat to a minimum and cover. Allow the porridge to simmer gently for 10 minutes.
2.   Stir in the salt, cover the pan once again and continue to simmer for a further 10 minutes until the porridge is cooked.
3.   Divide the porridge between 4 warmed bowls, sprinkle with whisky and sugar and dot with butter or douse with cream.

BREAKFAST BURGERS

THE COCKLE WARREN
Hayling Island, Hampshire
Diane & David Skelton

.

Liver and bacon burgers flavoured with sage. Serve Breakfast Burgers as an alternative to sausages on a traditional British Breakfast plate, or in a warm bun with mustard and ketchup as a hot snack.

Serves 6

500 g (1 lb) lean pork, minced
200 g (8 oz) unsmoked bacon, minced
100 g (4 oz) pig's liver, minced
1 onion, finely chopped
5 ml (1 tsp) chopped sage
2.5 ml (½ tsp) grated nutmeg
1 egg, beaten
wholemeal flour for coating
oil for frying

1. In a bowl, mix together all the ingredients. Divide the mixture into 6 and, using floured hands, shape into burgers or rissoles. Coat the burgers in flour.
2. Heat the oil in a frying pan and fry the burgers for approximately 10–15 minutes until browned on both sides. Serve immediately.

SAVOURY KIDNEYS

THE COCKLE WARREN
Hayling Island, Hampshire

Diane & David Skelton

.

Kidneys braised in a rich Madeira or sherry sauce, served on toast.

Serves 6

25 g (1 oz) butter
15 ml (1 tbsp) olive oil
1 large onion, thinly sliced
12 lamb's kidneys
flour for dusting
seasoning
200 g (8 oz) mushrooms
125 ml (5 fl oz) Madeira or sherry
125 ml (5 fl oz) good beef stock (see page 200)
15 g (½ oz) chopped parsley
pinch of grated nutmeg

To serve:
6 slices toast
chopped parsley

1. Heat the butter and the olive oil together in a saucepan, add the onion, cover and cook gently for 10 minutes until the onion is transparent.
2. Remove any fat and skin that is still around the kidneys and slice in half. Snip out the white cores with scissors, rinse and pat dry on kitchen paper. Slice into chunks and dust with flour and seasoning.
3. Add the kidneys and mushrooms to the pan, stir and cook for 3–4 minutes until the kidneys are sealed and the mushrooms softened.
4. Stir the Madeira, stock, parsley and nutmeg into the pan. Bring to the boil and allow to simmer for 10 minutes until the kidneys are cooked and tender, and the sauce has thickened.
5. Taste and adjust the seasoning before spooning onto toast and serving, sprinkled with chopped parsley.

SMOKED HADDOCK, MUSHROOM & SESAME COCOTTES

COMMODORE HOTEL
Weston-super-Mare, Avon

J. Stoakes with chef Paul Evans

.

Fillets of smoked haddock baked with sliced mushrooms, dill, eggs and milk, topped with sesame seeds. Serve with granary bread.

Serves 4

25 g (1 oz) butter
500 g (1 lb) smoked haddock fillets, skinned
100 g (4 oz) mushrooms, sliced
15 g (½ oz) chopped dill
seasoning
2 eggs
500 ml (1 pint) milk
25 g (1 oz) sesame seeds

To serve:
chopped parsley
granary bread

1. Preheat the oven to 220°C (425°F) mark 7.
2. Butter 4 individual cocotte dishes, large ovenproof bowls or ramekins and place on a baking sheet for ease of handling.
3. Cut the haddock into chunks and divide between the 4 dishes. Top with the mushrooms, dill and seasoning.
4. In a jug, beat the eggs into the milk with a fork, then pour over the fish.
5. Bake the cocottes in the preheated oven for 10 minutes. Sprinkle the top of each dish with an even layer of sesame seeds and return to the oven for 5–10 minutes until the sauce has set and the sesame seeds have turned golden.
6. Serve immediately, sprinkled with chopped parsley and accompanied by fresh granary bread.

KEDGEREE

CRINGLETIE HOUSE HOTEL
Peebles, Borders

Stanley & Aileen Maguire

.

A traditional breakfast dish of spiced smoked haddock, rice and eggs. Kedgeree can be successfully reheated in a bowl, set over a pan of hot water, or in the microwave.

Serves 6

600 g (1¼ lb) smoked haddock or cod
1 bay leaf
50 g (2 oz) butter
50 ml (2 fl oz) olive oil
1 onion, chopped
5 ml (1 tsp) curry powder (plus extra to taste)
2.5 ml (½ tsp) turmeric
250 g (10 oz) brown rice, cooked
1 canned pimento, chopped
3 eggs, hard-boiled, peeled and chopped
seasoning

To serve:
30 ml (2 tbsp) chopped parsley
2 lemons, cut into wedges

1. Place the haddock and bay leaf in a saucepan and barely cover with water. Bring to the boil, then reduce the heat and poach for 10 minutes until the fish is cooked. Drain and leave to cool slightly. Remove the skin and large bones from the fish and flake into chunks.
2. In a large saucepan, melt the butter and oil together. Add the onion and fry until soft but not browned. Stir in the curry powder and turmeric and cook for 1 minute.
3. Add the rice to the pan and stir to coat evenly with spice. Add the fish, pimento and chopped eggs. Heat gently, stirring constantly until all the ingredients are piping hot.
4. Taste and correct the seasoning. Spoon onto warmed plates, sprinkle liberally with parsley, dot with wedges of lemon and serve immediately.

STARTERS & SOUPS

STILTON & PORT PÂTÉ

BRENTWOOD HOTEL
Rotherham, Yorkshire

James Lister

.

A port-rich cheese and fruit pâté. Vary the fruit and vegetable ingredients to produce interesting results. For example, chopped tomatoes, cucumber, pineapple, peaches or nuts could be used.

Serves 8–10

500 g (1 lb) assorted hard cheese, including at least 25% Stilton
½ apple, peeled
½ small onion
½ red pepper
1 stick celery
125 ml (5 fl oz) port
5 ml (1 tsp) Worcestershire Sauce
125 g (5 oz) butter, softened

To serve:
salad garnish
Melba toast or oatcakes

1. Mince together the cheese, apple, onion, red pepper and celery, or process until they form small lumps in the food processor (it will be necessary to do this in batches).
2. In a bowl, stir the port, Worcestershire Sauce and butter into the cheese until there are no visible lumps of butter.
3. Press the pâté into a terrine mould or small individual ramekins and chill for at least 2 hours.
4. Serve with salad garnish and hot Melba toast or oatcakes.

PORT & BEAN PÂTÉ

THE OLD FORGE RESTAURANT
Newmill on Teviot, Borders

Bill & Margaret Irving

·

A vegetarian bean and herb pâté deliciously flavoured with port.

Serves 6–8

250 g (10 oz) red kidney beans
100 g (4 oz) butter
2 cloves garlic, crushed
30 ml (2 tbsp) chopped mixed herbs
juice of ½ lemon
2.5 ml (½ tsp) cayenne pepper
seasoning
100 ml (4 fl oz) port

To serve:
fresh herb sprigs
sticks celery
fresh granary bread

1.   Soak the kidney beans overnight, then drain.
2.   In a pan of boiling water, cook the kidney beans, boiling vigorously for 10 minutes, then simmering for 40 minutes until tender. Drain and reserve some of the cooking liquid.
3.   While the beans are warm, process to a smooth paste with all the other ingredients in a liquidiser or food processor. Add as much of the cooking liquid as necessary to obtain a smooth consistency.
4.   Spoon into individual ramekins and chill for at least 1 hour. Garnish with fresh herbs and serve with sticks of celery and hunks of fresh granary bread.

SWEET FRUIT & CHEESE PÂTÉ WITH OATCAKES

THE WOODLAND COTTAGE
Geddes Village, Nairn

Ian & Diane Scally

·

A cream cheese and dried fruit pâté, laced with brandy or sherry. This pâté will mature, tasting even better the day after preparation.

Serves 8–10

250 g (10 oz) mixed dried fruit, diced (dates, figs, sultanas, apricots, apple, pear, mango, for example)
15 ml (1 tbsp) fresh root ginger, grated and blanched
15 ml (1 tbsp) dried coconut strips, NOT desiccated flakes
45–60 ml (3–4 tbsp) sherry, brandy or coconut liqueur
15 ml (1 tbsp) double cream
300 g (12 oz) cream cheese
seasoning
butter for greasing

To serve:
salad garnish
oatcakes

1.   In a bowl, soak the fruit, ginger and coconut in the sherry, brandy or liqueur for 3 hours until the fruit is plump. If time is short, swell the fruit by heating it in the alcohol in a pan, simmer for 10 minutes, then leave to cool.
2.   In a bowl, beat together the cream and cream cheese, and fold in the soaked fruit. Taste and season.
3.   Lightly butter a 15 cm (6 inch) loose-bottomed round cake tin or 500 g (1 lb) loaf tin.
4.   Spoon the cheese mixture into the prepared tin, spread flat and chill thoroughly.
5.   Remove the pâté from the tin, garnish with salad and serve with oatcakes.

PUMPKIN TERRINE WITH A SAUCE OF PICKLED CHERRIES

THE DENBIGH ARMS HOTEL
Lutterworth, Leicestershire

Mr & Mrs Eric Stephens

.

Slices of delicately flavoured pumpkin terrine, served surrounded by a sharp, creamy, cherry sauce. This terrine can be eaten hot or cold, but the sauce tastes best when freshly made and still warm.

Serves 8

butter for greasing
1 kg (2 lb) pumpkin, peeled, seeded and cubed
5 eggs (size 4)
5 ml (1 tsp) grated nutmeg
seasoning

For the sauce:
600 ml (1¼ pints) double cream
30 ml (2 tbsp) raspberry vinegar
15 ml (1 tbsp) sweet white wine vinegar
25 g (1 oz) pickled cherries (available from good delicatessens)
seasoning

1. Preheat the oven to 180°C (350°F) mark 4. Grease a 750 ml (1½ pint) terrine, pâté dish or loaf tin.
2. Cook the pumpkin in boiling salted water until tender. Drain thoroughly in a colander.
3. Using a food processor or sieve, purée the pumpkin until smooth. Add the eggs, one at a time, with the nutmeg and seasoning.
4. Pour the mixture into the prepared mould, cover tightly with foil and place in a roasting tin, half filled with boiling water to form a waterbath. Bake in the oven for 1¼–1½ hours, until firm.
5. Once cooked, allow the terrine to cool slightly before carefully turning it out onto a serving plate.
6. To prepare the sauce, heat the cream, raspberry and white wine vinegars together in a pan. Bring to the boil, stirring, then allow to simmer until reduced to half the volume.
7. Away from the heat, add the pickled cherries to the sauce and allow the flavours to infuse for 2 minutes.
8. Season the sauce to taste and gently reheat if necessary before serving. Position a slice of terrine in the centre of each plate, flood the rim with sauce and serve.

CHICKEN & CREAM CHEESE TERRINE

HUNDRED HOUSE HOTEL
Norton, Shropshire

Henry, Sylvia & David Phillips with chef Anthony Baker

.

Chicken breasts, marinated in lime juice and brandy, baked in a pork, cream cheese and herb flavoured terrine.

Serves 10–12

4 chicken breasts, skinned and boned
juice of 2 limes
40 ml (1½ fl oz) brandy
200 g (8 oz) lean belly pork, minced
300 g (12 oz) lean, unsmoked rindless back bacon
4 cloves garlic, crushed
7.5 ml (1½ tsp) chopped sage
5 ml (1 tsp) chopped thyme
5 ml (1 tsp) chopped tarragon
7.5 ml (1½ tsp) chopped chives
7.5 ml (1½ tsp) chopped parsley
500 g (1 lb) cream cheese
2 eggs (size 4)
seasoning

To serve:
sprigs of fresh herbs
salad garnish

1.   Remove any fat and sinews from the chicken. In a bowl, marinate the chicken in the lime juice and brandy for 24 hours.
2.   Preheat the oven to 180°C (350°F) mark 4.
3.   In a frying pan, fry the belly pork until sealed and turning brown. Leave to cool.
4.   Run the blunt edge of a knife over each rasher of bacon to stretch the meat lengthways. Use the bacon to line a 1.5 litre (3 pint) terrine mould or loaf tin, allowing the ends of the rashers to hang over the edges of the mould.
5.   In a bowl, thoroughly mix together the garlic, herbs, fried pork, cream cheese, eggs and seasoning.
6.   One-third fill the prepared tin with the cheese mixture, lay the chicken breasts on top, then fill the terrine with the remaining cheese mix. Bring the free ends of bacon over the top of the terrine.

7. Tightly seal with foil, then stand the terrine in a roasting tin, half filled with boiling water to form a waterbath. Bake in the preheated oven for 1½ hours.
8. Leave to cool and rest for 1 hour after baking, then weight the top of the terrine overnight, to compress the meat. A couple of heavy cans work well to weigh down the terrine!
9. Garnish the terrine with herbs and serve in the mould, or turn the terrine out onto a serving plate and garnish with salad.

Note: To unmould a clinging terrine, run a knife around the edge of the mould, then dip the base of the tin in hot water, count to 10, remove from the water and upturn the terrine over a serving plate. Shake the plate and mould together until the terrine moves!

PARIS MUSHROOMS

THE DENBIGH ARMS HOTEL
Lutterworth, Leicestershire

Mr & Mrs Eric Stephens

Mushrooms in a creamy sauce, served hot on a crisp garlic roll.

Serves 4

1 clove garlic
100 g (4 oz) butter, softened
seasoning
2 French rolls or 4 slices of French bread
500 g (1 lb) Paris or other flat mushrooms
15 ml (1 tbsp) olive oil
30 ml (2 tbsp) white wine
30 ml (2 tbsp) mushroom ketchup
250 ml (10 fl oz) double cream

To serve:
15 g (½ oz) chopped parsley

1. Crush the garlic into the softened butter, season and mix together.
2. Halve the rolls and spread the surface with the garlic butter, then bake in a hot oven for 2 minutes.
3. Sauté the mushrooms in the oil until soft. Add the white wine, mushroom ketchup and stir together.
4. Add the cream, heat the mixture through and season to taste.
5. Serve half a roll per person, topped with the mushrooms and sauce, generously sprinkled with chopped parsley.

CHAMPIGNONS à la PÊCHEUR

SEAFARERS RESTAURANT
West Looe, Cornwall

Mr & Mrs C.J. Smith with chef Mrs A. Jones

.

Mushrooms flamed in brandy, served in a cream and crab meat sauce.

Serves 6

60 ml (4 tbsp) vegetable oil
175 g (7 oz) shallots, chopped
4 cloves garlic, crushed
500 g (1 lb) button mushrooms
seasoning
60 ml (4 tbsp) brandy
250 ml (10 fl oz) double cream
100 g (4 oz) white crab meat

To serve:
chopped parsley
Melba toast or large croûtons

1. Heat the oil in a large non-stick frying pan and gently cook the shallots and garlic for 1 minute, then add the mushrooms. Season and continue to cook over a gentle heat, stirring until the mushrooms are tender but not floppy. The mushrooms will absorb all the fat as they hit the pan, but keep stirring and they will cook in the dry heat.
2. Increase the heat, add the brandy and flame. Stir in the cream (this will extinguish the flames) and continue to cook until the sauce thickens. Taste and correct the seasoning.
3. Stir in the crab meat and transfer to warmed serving plates.
4. Sprinkle with parsley and serve with toast or croûtons.

CARDAMOM CIDER MUSHROOMS

THE KITCHEN
Polperro, Cornwall

Ian & Vanessa Bateson

.

Mushrooms cooked in cider sauce, flavoured with cardamom and set on slices of garlic toast. When entertaining, prepare the mushroom sauce in advance, then reheat and spoon over the hot, buttered toast at the last minute. Cardamom seeds are best crushed in a pestle and mortar.

Serves 4

45 ml (3 tbsp) olive oil
15 ml (1 tbsp) lemon juice
150 ml (6 fl oz) medium cider
12 cardamom pods, seeds removed and crushed
300 g (12 oz) button mushrooms, thickly sliced
4 slices French bread
25 g (1 oz) butter, softened
2 cloves garlic, crushed
5 ml (1 tsp) chopped parsley
seasoning

To serve:
4 sprigs of fresh coriander

1.   Place the oil, lemon juice, cider, cardamom seeds and mushrooms in a large saucepan. Stir all the ingredients together and bring to the boil, cover and remove from the heat.
2.   While the mushrooms are cooking, heat the grill and toast the bread until golden.
3.   Mix together the butter, garlic, parsley and seasoning. Spread the garlic butter over the piping hot toast, so the butter melts into the bread.
4.   Place a slice of toast in the base of a warm soup bowl and top with a spoonful of hot mushrooms and sauce. Garnish with sprigs of fresh coriander and serve.

MEXICAN WILD MUSHROOMS

THE NORFOLK HOUSE RESTAURANT & HOTEL
Taplow, Berkshire

Clive Allen-Stanton with chef Vincent Vassalio

.

Wild mushrooms in a very hot chilli, garlic and dry sherry sauce. If wild mushrooms are unavailable, ordinary button mushrooms can be used instead.

Serves 4

45 ml (3 tbsp) olive oil
500 g (1 lb) wild mushrooms (oyster, chestnut or as available)
4 cloves garlic, crushed
4 dried chillies, crumbled
10 ml (2 tsp) flour
5 ml (1 tsp) tomato purée
juice of 1 lemon
60 ml (4 tbsp) dry sherry
10 drops Worcestershire Sauce
100 ml (4 fl oz) fish stock (see page 200)
200 ml (8 fl oz) chicken stock (see page 201)
seasoning

To serve:
chopped parsley
garlic bread

1. Heat the oil in a deep-sided saucepan and fry the mushrooms, garlic and chilli for 2–3 minutes.
2. Stir in the flour and tomato purée, then gradually add the lemon juice, sherry, Worcestershire Sauce, fish and chicken stock. Stir to mix thoroughly. Bring to the boil and simmer for 5 minutes or until the mushrooms are soft. Taste and adjust seasoning.
3. Ladle into warmed shallow individual dishes and sprinkle with parsley before serving with hot garlic bread.

SPINACH & MUSHROOM TIMBALES WITH HERB & SOUR CREAM SAUCE

FLACKLEY ASH HOTEL
Peasmarsh, near Rye, Sussex

Clive & Jeanie Bennett

.

A delicate mix of spinach and mushrooms set in egg custard, surrounded by a sharp, fresh herb sauce. Spinach and mushroom timbales can be eaten either hot or cold.

Serves 6

For the timbales:
25 g (1 oz) butter
300 g (12 oz) mushrooms, sliced
500 g (1 lb) spinach
4 eggs
125 ml (5 fl oz) milk
125 ml (5 fl oz) chicken stock
seasoning

For the sauce:
250 ml (10 fl oz) soured cream
90 ml (6 tbsp) lemon juice
90 ml (6 tbsp) chopped mixed fresh herbs (mint, basil, chives and parsley, for example)
seasoning

To serve:
sprigs of fresh herbs

1. Preheat the oven to 180°C (350°F) mark 4. Lightly grease 6 ramekin dishes with half the butter.
2. Place the sliced mushrooms in a pan with the remaining butter and fry until tender.
3. Trim and wash the spinach. Cook in a large pan, without any added water, until tender. Drain and squeeze out any excess liquid.
4. In a liquidiser or food processor, purée the spinach and mushrooms together, then leave to cool slightly.
5. Stir the eggs into the cooled purée (make sure it is cool or the eggs will scramble as you add them), followed by the milk, chicken stock and seasoning.
6. Ladle the mixture into the prepared dishes and cover tightly with foil. Arrange the ramekins in a roasting tin, half filled with boiling water to form a waterbath. Bake in the preheated oven for 30–40 minutes until firm to the touch.
7. Prepare the sauce by mixing all the ingredients together (the herbs must be very finely chopped or the sauce will have a rough texture), taste and correct the seasoning.
8. To serve, allow the timbales to stand for 2 minutes once cooked, run a knife around the edge of the moulds and carefully turn out onto individual plates. Pour a little of the sauce around each timbale and garnish with sprigs of fresh herbs.

CAMEMBERT FRITTERS

LONG'S RESTAURANT
Truro, Cornwall

Ian & Ann Long

.

Camembert-flavoured fried nuggets, coated in breadcrumbs and sesame seeds. Although easy to prepare, allow 2 days to produce this dish. Fry the fritters in advance and reheat in the oven to avoid hot oil smells wafting from the kitchen when entertaining.

Serves 8

100 g (4 oz) butter
75 g (3 oz) flour
350 ml (14 fl oz) milk
200 g (8 oz) Camembert, without the rind, chopped
6 egg yolks
10 ml (2 tsp) coarse grain mustard
pinch of grated nutmeg
butter for greasing
flour for coating
1–2 large eggs, lightly beaten
salt
200 g (8 oz) brown breadcrumbs
50 g (2 oz) sesame seeds
oil for frying

To serve:
lettuce, shredded

1.   First prepare a white sauce. Melt the butter in a saucepan, stir in the flour to form a roux and cook for 2 minutes until sandy in texture. Gradually stir in the milk and bring to the boil. Simmer for 2 minutes.
2.   In a blender, process together the chopped Camembert and egg yolks until well mixed, spoon into the white sauce and heat, stirring, until the cheese has dissolved. Take the pan off the heat and stir in the mustard and nutmeg.
3.   Line a shallow baking tray with clingfilm and brush with a little melted butter. Pour the cheese mixture into the prepared tin and leave to cool and set overnight.
4.   Roll the mixture into 2.5 cm (1 inch) balls, then press with the fingertips to flatten into rounds 1.25 cm (½ inch) high.
5.   Prepare the coating mixtures in 3 bowls set side by side. Put the flour in one, the egg and salt mixed together in the second and the breadcrumbs and sesame seeds, tossed together, in the third.

6. Dip each Camembert piece in flour, coat with the egg and then with breadcrumb mix. Lay the coated balls on greaseproof paper and chill for at least an hour, or, better still, overnight.

7. Heat 1.25 cm (½ inch) of oil in a large frying pan and fry the fritters, a few at a time, until they are crisp and light brown, turning once. Drain on kitchen paper and serve hot, on a bed of lettuce.

BRIE & MANGO MONEYPURSES

FROGGIES WINE BAR AND RESTAURANT
Knaphill, Surrey

Robin & Debbie de Winton

.

Flaky filo pastry bags filled with creamy Brie and fresh mango slices.

Serves 8

200 g (8 oz) ripe Brie, rind removed
1 ripe mango, peeled, stoned and cut into chunks
40 ml (8 tsp) mango chutney
butter for greasing
8 sheets filo pastry
75 g (3 oz) butter, melted

To serve:
salad garnish

1. First prepare the filling for quick assembly of the moneypurses. Cut the Brie into 8 equal pieces, divide the mango pieces into 8 piles, open the jar of mango chutney and have a clean teaspoon ready.

2. Heat the oven to 200°C (400°F) mark 6. Grease a baking sheet.

3. Now, working quickly so the pastry does not dry out, uncover the first sheet of pastry. Brush melted butter over the sheet, cut in half. Place one half over the top of the other so the buttered side meets un-buttered. Cut the sheet in half (in the opposite direction from your first cut) and bring this double layer over the top of the first. Set this over the base sheets, forming a cross shape.

4. Place a portion of cheese, mango and mango chutney in the centre of the pastry. Gather up and seal the package over the filling by pressing the pastry together firmly, allowing the edges to frill out.

5. Generously paint the outside with melted butter before placing on the prepared baking sheet, and repeating for the remaining purses.

6. Bake in the preheated oven for 10–12 minutes or until the pastry is crisp and golden. Serve piping hot, with a salad garnish.

TOURTES OF PIGEON MOUSSELINE WITH FRESH HERBS

CHELWOOD HOUSE HOTEL
Chelwood, Avon
Jill & Rudi Birk with chef Michael Taylor

.

A delicate, herb-flavoured pigeon mousseline, sandwiched between puff pastry circles, served with a Madeira, juniper berry and redcurrant sauce. As an alternative to pigeon, use minced chicken meat to prepare the mousseline.

Serves 4

For the pastry:
300 g (12 oz) puff pastry
1 egg, lightly beaten

For the mousseline:
butter for greasing
200 g (8 oz) minced pigeon
2 sprigs tarragon
1 sprig thyme
3 egg whites
seasoning
200 ml (8 fl oz) double cream

For the sauce:
15 g (½ oz) butter
1 small onion, finely chopped
15 g (½ oz) flour
600 ml (1¼ pints) pigeon or chicken stock
200 ml (8 fl oz) Madeira
10 ml (2 tsp) juniper berries
30 ml (2 tbsp) redcurrant jelly
seasoning

1.   Preheat the oven to 220°C (425°F) mark 7.
2.   Roll out the pastry as thinly as possible and, using plain-edged pastry cutters, cut out 4 circles 10 cm (4 inches) in diameter, and 4 circles 7.5 cm (3 inches) in diameter. Arrange all the circles on a baking sheet and chill for 10 minutes.
3.   Lightly run a knife over the surface of the smaller pastry circles, creating lines radiating from the centre like the spokes of a wheel. This

will form a pattern on the surface of the cooked pastry. Brush the pastry with egg and bake in the preheated oven for 15 minutes until golden.

4.   Now prepare the mousselines. Lightly butter 4 heatproof tea cups or ramekin dishes.

5.   In a food processor, purée the pigeon, tarragon and thyme until very smooth. Chill the purée thoroughly. Return the mixture to the processor and whizz in the seasoning and egg whites. Chill once more before slowly beating in the cream.

6.   Reduce the oven heat to 180°C (250°F) mark 4.

7.   Spoon the mousseline mixture into the prepared moulds, and stand in a roasting tin, half filled with boiling water to form a waterbath. Cover the tray with foil and bake for 20 minutes or until the mousses feel firm. Return the pastry circles, covered to avoid burning, to the hot oven during the last few minutes of baking to warm through.

8.   While the mousses are cooking, prepare the sauce by melting the butter in a saucepan and frying the finely chopped onion for 5 minutes until transparent. Stir in the flour, followed by the stock, Madeira, juniper berries and redcurrant jelly. Bring to the boil and simmer for 5–10 minutes until considerably thickened and reduced. Sieve to remove the onion and keep warm.

9.   Run a knife around the edge of each cooked mousse mould. Set the 4 larger rings of pastry in the centre of 4 warmed plates and carefully turn the mousselines out onto them, then cap with a smaller pastry circle. Flood a little sauce around each mousseline tourte and serve immediately.

DEEP-FRIED VEGETARIAN PARCELS

THE LORD NELSON & CARRIAGES RESTAURANT
Marshfield, Wiltshire

Roy & Jeanette Lane with chef Paul Cuss

·

Hot puff pastry parcels filled with spinach, mushrooms and cashew nuts, served with a sweet port, redcurrant and pine kernel dip and garnished with slices of avocado and a crisp salad. As the parcels fry they expand considerably in the hot fat, so it is better only to cook a few at a time, keeping them in the oven until ready to serve. Experiment with other parcel fillings; for example, minced lamb with cumin and mint, or cream cheese flavoured with chopped fresh or canned pineapple.

Serves 6

For the parcels:
200 g (8 oz) puff pastry
50 g (2 oz) cooked spinach, thoroughly drained
25 g (1 oz) mushrooms, finely diced
15 g (½ oz) cashew nuts, roughly chopped
pinch of grated nutmeg
seasoning
1 egg yolk, lightly beaten
oil for frying

For the dip:
75 g (3 oz) redcurrant jelly
25 ml (1 fl oz) port
15 g (½ oz) pine kernels
seasoning

To serve:
1 avocado, peeled, stoned and sliced
crisp salad

1. Divide the pastry in 2. On a floured surface, roll out both pieces of pastry until they form 2 thin square sheets of approximately the same shape and size.
2. Mix the spinach, mushrooms, cashew nuts, nutmeg and seasoning together in a bowl.
3. Dot the filling mixture in 6 spots over one pastry sheet, to form a grid, leaving equal spaces between each pile of filling. Brush egg between each dot and lay the second sheet of pastry over the top. Using the side of the hand, press the pastry together to form neat filled squares, like large ravioli. Cut the squares apart using a knife or pastry wheel.
4. Refrigerate the squares for 30 minutes.
5. Melt the redcurrant jelly in a small saucepan, add the port and pine kernels, stir until mixed and season to taste.
6. Heat the oil in a deep fat fryer or high-sided frying pan. Fry the parcels for 10 minutes until golden brown, then drain thoroughly on kitchen paper.
7. Arrange a bed of lettuce leaves on individual serving plates. Place a vegetable parcel to one side of the lettuce, with a little hot redcurrant dip in a small ramekin on the other side, or drizzle some dip over the top of the parcel. Garnish with a fan of avocado slices and serve.

SAUTÉ CHICKEN LIVERS ON TOAST

FASGANEOIN HOTEL
Pitlochry, Tayside

The Turk Family

.

Chicken livers in a creamy, nutty sauce, set on a round of crisp toast, garnished with orange segments.

Serves 4

½ Spanish onion, diced
15 ml (1 tbsp) olive oil
200 g (8 oz) chicken livers
15 ml (1 tbsp) flour
25 g (1 oz) cashew nuts, finely ground
65 ml (2½ fl oz) single cream
2.5 ml (½ tsp) chopped sage
seasoning
15 g (½ oz) butter
1 large or 2 medium oranges, peeled and sliced
4 slices toast, cut into large circles using a pastry cutter

1. In a frying pan, fry the onion in the oil until transparent. Remove the onion using a slotted spoon and keep to one side.
2. Cut the chicken livers into bite-sized pieces. Dust with the flour, shaking off any excess, then fry in the remaining oil for 5 minutes, stirring once or twice.
3. Return the onions to the pan, sprinkle on the nuts, stir in the cream, sage and seasoning. Heat gently.
4. In a separate frying pan, melt the butter and fry the orange slices until hot and glazed.
5. Arrange the toast circles on warm plates, pile with the hot livers and garnish with the orange slices. Serve immediately.

LE PETIT PAIN SAUCE PORTO

LES QUAT' SAISONS – 1977

Raymond Blanc

.

A light mousse of chicken livers served with a port sauce. This recipe
was served in Raymond Blanc's first restaurant – Les Quat' Saisons,
Summertown, Oxford – which was Les Routiers recommended.

Serves 4

For the mousse:
125 g (5 oz) chicken or duck livers
100 ml (4 fl oz) milk for soaking
100 ml (4 fl oz) water for soaking
1 egg
1 egg yolk
125 ml (5 fl oz) milk
125 ml (5 fl oz) whipping cream
seasoning
butter for greasing

For the port sauce:
65 g (2½ oz) butter
3 shallots, chopped
3 tomatoes, skinned, seeded and chopped
½ bay leaf
1 sprig thyme
200 g (8 oz) button mushrooms, sliced
½ clove garlic
100 ml (4 fl oz) dry Madeira
100 ml (4 fl oz) ruby port
100 ml (4 fl oz) water
100 ml (4 fl oz) cream
seasoning

To serve:
1 tomato, skinned, seeded and diced
4 sprigs fresh chervil

1.   First prepare the mousse. Remove the gall from the livers and, if
they are stained, soak them in the milk and water for 12 hours. Drain,
rinse and pat dry. Throw away the soaking liquid.
2.   Preheat the oven to 170°C (325°F) mark 3.

3. In a food processor, mix together the livers, egg and egg yolk. Add the milk, cream and seasoning, process thoroughly, then pass the mixture through a fine sieve.

4. Grease 4 × 10 cm (4 inch) diameter ramekins thoroughly and fill with the prepared mousse mixture. Stand the ramekins in a roasting tin, half-filled with boiling water to form a waterbath, and cover loosely with foil. Bake in the preheated oven for 25 minutes.

5. Meanwhile, prepare the port sauce. In a saucepan, melt half the butter and sweat the shallots for 5 minutes until transparent. Add the tomatoes, bay leaf, thyme, button mushrooms and garlic. Cook for a further 5 minutes.

6. Add the Madeira, port and water to the pan, bring to the boil and allow to simmer until reduced to half the volume. In a blender or food processor, liquidise the sauce, then pass through a fine sieve into a saucepan.

7. Add the cream to the sauce and bring to the boil. Cut the remaining butter into small knobs and, using a balloon whisk, whisk into the sauce. Taste and season.

8. In a small pan, gently heat the diced tomato garnish.

9. Run a knife around the edge of the cooked mousse moulds and turn out onto the centre of 4 warmed plates. Place a spoonful of warm tomato dice on top of each mousse and crown with a sprig of chervil. Pour a little sauce around the base of each mousse and serve.

PAKURA

THE VERANDAH RESTAURANT
Edinburgh
Wali Tasar Uddin with chef Kaisar Miah

Deep-fried spicy vegetable balls. Serve small pakura with drinks as an unusual aperitif. Gram flour is a fine yellow flour ground from the gram pulse. It is very rich in food value and can be bought from most ethnic grocers.

Serves 4–5

2.5 ml (½ tsp) cumin, ground
2.5 ml (½ tsp) turmeric
2 hot chillies, diced finely
50 g (2 oz) chopped fresh coriander
½ green pepper, chopped finely
1 potato, peeled and cut into very small dice
2 large onions, peeled and cut into very small dice
1 egg
5 ml (1 tsp) salt
150 g (6 oz) gram flour
oil for frying

To serve:
salt
1 lemon, cut into wedges
chopped coriander

1. In a large bowl, mix together the cumin, turmeric, chillies, coriander, green pepper, potato, onions, egg and salt.
2. Stir the flour into the mixture, then add 45–60 ml (3–4 tbsp) cold water to make a gluey consistency.
3. Heat the oil in a deep fat fryer or heavy-based saucepan. When hot, drop squash-ball sized spoonfuls of mixture into the oil. (This is most easily done by using one spoon to slide a spoonful of mixture off another into the hot oil.)
4. Fry the pakura for 10–15 minutes until golden brown, drain thoroughly on kitchen paper, sprinkle with salt and serve while hot, garnished with lemon wedges and chopped coriander.

PEACH ESQUIRE

OLD HALL HOTEL
Buxton, Derbyshire

Mrs Louise Potter with chef J.R. Lath

.

Fried slices of breadcrumb-coated fresh peach, served with a brandy, cream and garlic sauce. Use slices of mango or plum to prepare this dish, when peaches are out of season.

Serves 4

1 egg, lightly beaten
100 ml (4 fl oz) milk
2 firm fresh peaches, halved
50 g (2 oz) flour
100 g (4 oz) fine white breadcrumbs
75 g (3 oz) butter
1 small onion, finely chopped
2 cloves garlic, crushed
1 small red pepper, finely chopped
8 small mushrooms, thinly sliced
4 ripe tomatoes, peeled and chopped
30 ml (2 tbsp) brandy
seasoning
100 ml (4 fl oz) double cream

To serve:
15 ml (1 tbsp) chopped parsley

1. In a saucepan, gently heat together the egg and milk until bubbles start to appear on the surface. Remove the pan from the heat.
2. Remove the stones from the halved peaches and cut each half into 3 segments. Spear the segments onto a fork then dip each in the flour, followed by the egg mixture and lastly the breadcrumbs to coat completely. Press the crumbs on to ensure a firm coating.
3. Melt the butter in a large frying pan and fry the coated peaches for 2 minutes until golden brown on one side. Add the onion, garlic, pepper and mushrooms to the pan and carefully turn over the peach slices. As soon as the second sides of the peaches are cooked and golden, add the chopped tomatoes and brandy. Season to taste, stir in the cream and boil, allowing the sauce to thicken slightly.
4. Spoon onto warmed plates, sprinkle with parsley and serve.

STILTON-STUFFED PEACHES WITH ORANGE MAYONNAISE

NETHERWOOD HOTEL
Grange-over-Sands, Cumbria
Messrs J.D. & M.P. Fallowfield

.

Peaches filled with Stilton, coated in an orange-flavoured mayonnaise. Prepare this dish with ripe pears when peaches are out of season.

Serves 4

4 large fresh peaches
75 g (3 oz) Stilton, grated
grated zest of 1 orange
30 ml (2 tbsp) fresh orange juice
100 ml (4 fl oz) mayonnaise
seasoning

To serve:
salad of endive, watercress, little gem lettuce and cucumber
2 eggs, hard-boiled, peeled and quartered (optional)
chopped parsley

1. Plunge the peaches into a bowl of boiling water for 2–3 minutes. Drain and refresh in a bowl of iced water. The fruit should now be easy to peel.
2. Cut the skinned peaches in half and remove the stones, then press the Stilton into the stone cavity.
3. Stir the orange zest and juice into the mayonnaise, season.
4. Arrange the salad on 4 × 20 cm (8 inch) plates and top with the filled peaches, then chill.
5. Spoon orange mayonnaise over the peach halves, garnish with the egg quarters and chopped parsley and serve.

PEARS & PROSCIUTTO

LE GRANDGOUSIER
Brighton, Sussex
Mr L.M. Harris with chef Mr. O.P. Godfrey
·

Pears and cured ham, complemented by a wonderful honey vinaigrette.

Serves 4

2 ripe (but not soft) pears, peeled
juice of ½ lemon
4 wafer-thin slices of prosciutto
12 black olives
10 ml (2 tsp) chopped parsley

For the vinaigrette:
pinch of salt
2.5 ml (½ tsp) Dijon mustard
5 ml (1 tsp) honey
1 clove garlic, sliced
50 ml (2 fl oz) white wine vinegar
50 ml (2 fl oz) olive oil
50 ml (2 fl oz) grapeseed or peanut oil

1.   Using a teaspoon, scoop out the stalk and core of the pears. Halve and thinly slice, leaving each half slightly joined at the bulbous end. Fan out half a pear on each of 4 individual serving plates and sprinkle with the lemon juice to avoid discoloration.
2.   Arrange a slice of prosciutto at the other side of each plate, dot with the black olives and sprinkle with chopped parsley. Chill until ready to serve.
3.   Mix all the vinaigrette ingredients together in a screw-top jar and shake for 1 minute to blend. Spoon a little dressing over the pear and ham, serving the remaining sauce in an accompanying jug.

STUFFED PEPPER RINGS

THE WOODLAND COTTAGE
Geddes Village, Nairn
Ian & Diane Scally

.

Peppers, filled with a delicate apple and cream cheese mix. Alternative filling possibilities are endless. Add a little curry powder to the cheese, if you like spicy food, or a crushed clove of garlic and a dash of Worcestershire Sauce. Add 100 g (4 oz) of chopped prawns and a squeeze of lemon juice for a seafood pepper ring, or 25 g (1 oz) chopped walnuts and 1 diced avocado in place of the apple.

Serves 6–8

2 medium red peppers
2 medium green peppers
100 g (4 oz) Cheddar cheese, grated
200 g (8 oz) cream cheese
1 green apple
1 red apple
juice of ½ lemon
seasoning
15 ml (1 tbsp) chopped parsley

To serve:
salad garnish
brown bread

1. Slice the tops off the peppers, remove the seeds and any side filaments.
2. In a bowl, mix together the Cheddar and cream cheese until smooth.
3. Core, but do not peel, the apples. Cut into small dice and drop the apple pieces into a bowl containing the lemon juice. Turn the apples, to ensure all pieces are coated, to avoid discoloration.
4. Drain the apples, then stir into the cream cheese mixture, season and add the parsley.
5. Spoon the mixture into the peppers, pressing the filling down into the cavity to ensure it is completely filled. Refrigerate for 2–3 hours.
6. Slice the peppers carefully with a sharp knife, to expose a pepper ring with cream cheese central filling. Arrange 4–5 rings on each plate, alternating red and green pepper slices. Garnish with salad and serve with brown bread.

ARBROATH SMOKIES BAKED WITH CREAM

THE OLD FORGE RESTAURANT
Newmill on Teviot, Borders
Bill & Margaret Irving

.

Arbroath smokies baked with cream, cheese and lemon juice, topped with a tot of whisky. Serve double quantities, prepared in a large pie dish, with mashed potato as a main course.

Serves 4

2 Arbroath smokies
4 small tomatoes
seasoning
juice and grated zest of 1 lemon
100 g (4 oz) Cheddar cheese, grated
150 ml (6 fl oz) double cream
20 ml (4 tsp) whisky

1. Preheat the oven to 200°C (400°F) mark 6.
2. Skin, bone and flake the fish into 4 ramekin dishes.
3. Skin, seed and chop the tomatoes and add to the fish together with seasoning, lemon juice and zest. Mix thoroughly.
4. In a bowl, mix half the grated cheese with the cream and pour over the fish. Allow the cream and cheese to filter through the ramekin slightly, then sprinkle the remaining cheese over the top.
5. Bake in the preheated oven for 10–15 minutes until bubbling and golden on top. Sprinkle a little whisky over each ramekin and serve.

ARBROATH SEAWEED

MONTMORENCY RESTAURANT
Eton, Berkshire
Doreen Stanton with chef Nick Merkett

.

An unusual starter of Scottish seaweed with a rich prawn, cream and lemon sauce.

Serves 4

100 ml (4 fl oz) olive oil
250 g (10 oz) fresh Scottish seaweed (available from fishmongers)
8 spring onions, chopped
200 g (8 oz) prawns
juice and grated zest of 2 lemons
125 ml (5 fl oz) double cream

To serve:
1 bunch watercress
1 lemon, cut into wedges

1.   Heat half the oil in a large frying pan and, when very hot (nearly smoking), add the seaweed and cook until very crisp.
2.   In a separate pan, fry the onions with the prawns in the remaining oil over a gentle heat. Drain off excess oil, add the juice and zest of the lemons and simmer for 1 minute.
3.   Add the double cream to the prawn mixture, bring to the boil and cook until reduced to half volume.
4.   Drain excess oil from the seaweed and divide between 4 warm plates. Pour the sauce over the top and garnish with watercress and lemon wedges.

SMOKED SALMON PÂTÉ

LE GRANDGOUSIER
Brighton, Sussex

Mr L.M. Harris with chef Mr O.P. Godfrey

.

A delicate, creamy smoked salmon pâté that is very quick to make.

Serves 4

50 g (2 oz) butter, softened
15 ml (1 tbsp) olive oil
200 g (8 oz) smoked salmon pieces
30 ml (2 tbsp) lemon juice
60 ml (4 tbsp) double cream
2.5 ml (½ tsp) cayenne pepper
seasoning

1. Put the butter and oil into a food processor and cream together until smooth. Add the salmon and whizz until the salmon is reduced to a purée.
2. Add the lemon juice and blend, followed by the cream and cayenne pepper. Taste and correct seasoning if necessary, then chill until required.

SMOKED SALMON SCANDINAVIAN

THE CIDER PRESS RESTAURANT
Drybrook, Gloucestershire
Bernadette Fitzpatrick with chef Christopher Challener

Scrambled eggs, sitting on pumpernickel, topped with cornets of smoked salmon and cucumber.

Serves 4

25 g (1 oz) butter
4 slices pumpernickel or rye bread
mixed salad leaves (curly endive, chicory and watercress, for example)
30 ml (2 tbsp) walnut oil
200 g (8 oz) oak smoked salmon, sliced
seasoning
6 large free range eggs, lightly beaten
30 ml (2 tbsp) double cream
¼ cucumber, thinly sliced

1. Butter the pumpernickel, sparingly. Place each piece in the centre of a medium-sized plate.
2. Arrange the salad leaves around the edge of the bread and drizzle the walnut oil over the top.
3. Cut the smoked salmon into 12 strips and roll up to form small cornets.
4. Melt the remaining butter in a saucepan. Season the beaten eggs. Pour the eggs onto the hot butter and stir with a wooden spoon until thickened slightly, then stir in the double cream.
5. As soon as the scrambled eggs are cooked, spoon onto the pumpernickel and top with the salmon cornets and cucumber slices, arranged alternately around the mound of egg. Serve immediately while the egg is still piping hot.

GRAVAD LAX

HOTEL EILEAN IARMAIN
Isle of Skye

Iain Noble

.

Salmon cured with dill and sea salt, served with a mustard and vinegar sauce. Gravad lax always tastes especially good when washed down with a shot of ice cold schnapps!

Serves 8–10

1 kg (2 lb) middle cut fresh salmon
65 g (2½ oz) caster sugar
200 g (8 oz) chopped fresh dill
65 g (2½ oz) coarse sea salt
10 black peppercorns, roughly crushed

For the sauce:
30 ml (2 tbsp) German mustard
1 egg yolk
15 ml (1 tbsp) caster sugar
30 ml (2 tbsp) white wine vinegar
105 ml (7 tbsp) olive oil
15 ml (1 tbsp) chopped fresh dill
seasoning

To serve:
2 lemons, sliced or cut into wedges
sprigs of fresh dill
rye bread, spread with unsalted butter

1. Skin and fillet the salmon; you should be left with two large pieces. Wash and pat the fish dry with kitchen paper.
2. Rub the caster sugar into each of the 4 sides of the salmon fillets.
3. Sprinkle a third of the dill on the base of a shallow dish, and place one of the fish fillets on top. Sprinkle another third of the dill over the fish, together with half the sea salt and all the peppercorns. Cover with the remaining salmon fillet, the rest of the dill and salt.
4. Loosely place a piece of clingfilm over the fish then top with a heavily weighted wooden board or plate (a couple of cans act as excellent weights!).
5. Refrigerate for at least 48 hours (5 days maximum), turning the fish every 12 hours to spread the flavour evenly. While curing, the salmon will turn a much deeper pink – almost like smoked salmon –

and give off quite a quantity of oil; drain this each time you turn the fish.

6. Prepare the sauce by beating together the mustard, egg yolk, caster sugar and vinegar. Gradually add the oil – beating constantly – until the sauce has thickened and blended. Add the dill and season to taste.

7. Carve the cured salmon into paper-thin slices across the grain. Serve drizzled with mustard sauce, garnished with lemon and sprigs of fresh dill, accompanied by buttered rye bread.

PRAWNS 'SIENNA GORDA'

BRADFORD ARMS & RESTAURANT
Llanymynech, Shropshire
Michael & Ann Murphy

.

King prawns in a spicy orange marinade. Standard prawns could be used to prepare this recipe, although king prawns do have a wonderful flavour and texture which justifies the extra cost.

Serves 4

500 g (1 lb) cooked king prawns, peeled
45 ml (3 tbsp) orange flesh, chopped
45 ml (3 tbsp) chopped parsley
45 ml (3 tbsp) onion, finely chopped
45 ml (3 tbsp) red and green peppers, chopped
250 ml (10 fl oz) white wine
250 ml (10 fl oz) fresh orange juice
1 dash Tabasco
seasoning

To serve:
salad garnish
1 orange, sliced
sprigs of parsley

1. Mix all the ingredients together in a large bowl. Cover and chill for at least 30 minutes.

2. Divide the prawns and marinade between tall wine glasses or individual plates lined with salad. Garnish with slices of orange cut and shaped into twists, and sprigs of parsley. Serve chilled.

EASTERN SOLE FILLETS

TREWITHEN RESTAURANT
Lostwithiel, Cornwall

Mr & Mrs B.F. Rolls

·

Poached fillets of sole, filled with spiced cream cheese and coated with a tandoori crust, sliced and served cold.

Serves 4

For the filling:
1 small onion, finely chopped
1 clove garlic, crushed
15 g (½ oz) butter
100 g (4 oz) cream cheese
5 ml (1 tsp) cumin
5 ml (1 tsp) coriander seeds
2.5 ml (½ tsp) turmeric
1.25 cm (½ inch) fresh ginger, grated
10 ml (2 tsp) lemon juice
seasoning

For the crust:
oil for brushing
15–30 ml (1–2 tbsp) tandoori powder
5 ml (1 tsp) salt
4 × 150 g (6 oz) double fillets of sole, skinned

To serve:
mango chutney
salad garnish

1.   First prepare the cream cheese filling. In a pan, heat the onion, garlic and butter together for 10 minutes, until the onion is transparent. Allow to cool, then mix in the cheese.
2.   In a spice mill or coffee grinder, process all the spices to form a powder, add to the cheese mixture, with the lemon juice and seasoning to taste.
3.   Brush 4 sheets of greaseproof paper with oil, covering an area slightly bigger than the surface of each fillet. Evenly sprinkle the tandoori powder and salt over the oiled paper, then place the fillet of fish on top.
4.   Place a quarter of the filling on top of each fish. Spread into an even 'tube shape' along the length of the fish and roll up lengthwise,

inside the greaseproof paper, so the fish encloses the filling. Tightly twist the paper ends to secure the fish roll, forming a cracker shape.

5. Wrap the fish parcels in a clean tea towel or muslin cloth, securing the ends of each parcel with string.

6. Bring a pan of water to the boil. Carefully lower the fish into the pan and poach in simmering water for 10 minutes. Remove the fish from the hot water and leave to cool on a wire rack.

7. After 3–4 hours, when completely cold, remove the greaseproof paper and carefully slice each fillet into 4 or 5 pieces. Fan out to expose the filling and serve with mango chutney and salad.

FAGIOLI AL TONNO

NICODEMUS RESTAURANT
Chichester, West Sussex

Peter Bailey & Melvyn Marsh

.

A bean and tuna fish salad, flavoured with fresh basil, lemon and garlic.

Serves 6–8

200 g (8 oz) canned, or cooked dried white haricot beans
200 g (8 oz) canned, or cooked dried red kidney beans
200 g (8 oz) canned tuna fish
1 onion, finely chopped
1 green pepper, chopped
2 sticks celery, diced
60 ml (4 tbsp) olive oil
45 ml (3 tbsp) lemon juice
30 ml (2 tbsp) chopped basil
1 clove garlic, crushed
seasoning

To serve:
mixed lettuce leaves

1. Drain and rinse the beans. Drain the tuna fish.

2. Mix the beans, tuna, onion, pepper and celery in a large bowl.

3. Mix the oil, lemon juice, basil, garlic and seasoning together in a screw-top jar, and shake until well mixed. Pour the dressing over the tuna and bean mixture, then toss the salad to make sure all the ingredients are coated.

4. Chill thoroughly before serving on a bed of lettuce.

TROUT & PRAWN TERRINE

MILLMEAD COUNTRY HOTEL
Portesham, Dorset

Peter & Marion Cox

.

A layered terrine of creamed trout and prawns, served with French bread and horseradish mayonnaise.

Serves 6–8

2 trout
1 bay leaf
oil for greasing
15 ml (1 tbsp) chopped parsley
5 ml (1 tsp) chopped thyme
5 ml (1 tsp) snipped chives
2 eggs
20 ml (4 tsp) lemon juice
seasoning
200 g (8 oz) peeled prawns

To serve:
toast fingers or French bread
salad garnish
mayonnaise flavoured with horseradish sauce

1.   Place the trout and bay leaf in a saucepan, cover with water, bring to the boil and simmer for 5 minutes until the trout is cooked. Drain and leave the fish to cool slightly.
2.   Preheat the oven to 150°C (300°F) mark 2. Grease and line a 500 g (1 lb) loaf tin with greaseproof paper.
3.   Skin and bone the cooked trout, flaking the flesh into a liquidiser. Mix in the herbs, eggs, lemon juice and seasoning. Whizz until the mixture forms a smooth purée.
4.   Spread a third of the trout mixture over the base of the prepared tin, top with half the prawns, then another third of trout mix and the remaining prawns. Finally spread over the remaining trout mixture.
5.   Stand the tin in a roasting tray, half filled with boiling water to form a waterbath. Bake in the preheated oven for 30 minutes.
6.   Leave to cool, then turn out onto a serving dish. Serve chilled, sliced to show off the different layers, with toast, salad garnish and a little mayonnaise flavoured with horseradish sauce.

MARINER'S LEMONS

THE SCHOONER
Swansea, West Glamorgan

Raymond & Christine Parkman

.

A creamy mix of prawns, tuna and mayonnaise served in hollowed lemon 'cups'.

Serves 4

8 large lemons
100 g (4 oz) peeled prawns
100 g (4 oz) flaked tuna
1 onion, finely chopped
60 ml (4 tbsp) thick mayonnaise
60 ml (4 tbsp) sour cream
seasoning
pinch of paprika

To serve:
chopped parsley
iceberg lettuce, shredded
brown bread

1.   Slice the tops off the lemons. Using a melon baller or teaspoon, remove all the lemon flesh, catching the juice and flesh in a mixing bowl. Use scissors to snip off any awkward pieces of pith from the centre of the lemon.
2.   Remove pips and large pieces of pith from the lemon flesh and chop any large segments.
3.   Cut a small slice off the bottom of each lemon so it can stand up straight, but try not to break open the lemon 'cup' as you slice.
4.   Mix all the remaining ingredients with 120 ml (8 tbsp) of the lemon flesh and juice, taste, correct seasoning and add a little more of the lemon according to your palette.
5.   Pile the mixture into the lemon shells, chill thoroughly. Garnish with chopped parsley and serve 2 lemon 'cups' per person on a bed of shredded lettuce, with hunks of fresh brown bread.

AVOCADO ALASTAIR

ALASTAIR'S BISTRO
Leamington Spa, Warwickshire

Alan J. Reader

·

Chunks of avocado, sautéed with prawns, mushrooms and tomatoes, served hot in a cream and sherry sauce.

Serves 4

2 avocados
25 g (1 oz) butter
200 g (8 oz) mushrooms, sliced
2 tomatoes, skinned and chopped
seasoning
50 g (2 oz) cooked prawns, peeled
30 ml (2 tbsp) sherry
30 ml (2 tbsp) white wine
200 ml (8 fl oz) double cream

To serve:
chopped parsley
1 lemon, cut into wedges

1. Halve, skin and remove the stones from the avocado. Cut into chunks.
2. Melt the butter in a frying pan and, when hot, add the avocado, mushrooms and tomatoes. Season and cook for 2 minutes, stirring.
3. Add the prawns, sherry and wine and continue to cook while the liquids reduce for 2–3 minutes.
4. Add the cream to the pan, stir and continue to cook until the sauce thickens slightly. Taste and correct seasoning.
5. Spoon the avocado cream into individual hot bowls or plates and serve sprinkled with chopped parsley and garnished with lemon wedges.

SEAVIEW HOT CRAB RAMEKINS

SEAVIEW HOTEL
Seaview, Isle of Wight

Nicola & Nicholas Hayward

.

These creamy, hot crab and cheese ramekins taste best when made with freshly caught crab. For a less rich version of this dish, substitute a little white sauce for the thick cream.

Serves 4–6

500 g (1 lb) crab meat
250 ml (10 fl oz) thick double cream
100 g (4 oz) Cheddar cheese, grated
5–10 ml (1–2 tsp) dried mustard powder or mace
juice of ½ lemon
10 ml (2 tsp) anchovy essence
a few drops of chilli sauce
seasoning

To serve:
1 lemon, cut into wedges
brown rolls

1. Preheat the oven to 220°C (425°F) mark 7 or turn on the grill.
2. Mix the crab meat and cream together in a pan and heat gently. Add half the grated cheese, followed by all the remaining ingredients. Continue to heat until the cheese has melted and the mixture is hot and bubbling.
3. Pour the mixture into ramekin dishes and sprinkle the remaining cheese on top.
4. Brown in the hot oven or under the grill, and serve with wedges of lemon and fresh brown rolls.

AVOCADO & SEAFOOD CREAMS

WYNDHAM ARMS
Clearwell, Gloucestershire

John Stanford

·

Avocado, mashed with mayonnaise, cream and lemon juice, mixed with crab meat and diced peppers, served in its skin. For a change, try substituting a range of different seafood for the crab meat – tuna, prawns, or mussels, for example.

Serves 4

2 ripe avocados
30 ml (2 tbsp) lemon juice
75 g (3 oz) crab meat
30 ml (2 tbsp) diced red and green peppers
30 ml (2 tbsp) mayonnaise
125 ml (5 fl oz) double cream
pinch of chilli powder
seasoning
15 ml (1 tbsp) chopped parsley

To serve:
parsley sprigs
salad garnish
Melba toast or rye bread

1.   Halve the avocados and spoon out the flesh into a bowl, taking care to keep the skins intact.
2.   Mash the avocado with the lemon juice, stir in the crab meat, peppers and mayonnaise.
3.   Whip the cream until it forms soft peaks, then stir into the mixture.
4.   Add chilli powder, seasoning and parsley.
5.   Pile the mixture back into the skins, top with sprigs of parsley and serve chilled, garnished with salad and accompanied by Melba toast or rye bread.

MUSHROOMS & MUSSELS AU GRATIN

THE COCKLE WARREN
Hayling Island, Hampshire
Diane & David Skelton

.

Individual pots of mussels baked in a creamy mushroom sauce, with a crisp cheese topping.

Serves 4–6

50 g (2 oz) butter
200 g (8 oz) mushrooms, washed and sliced
200 g (8 oz) mussels (use thawed, shelled plump frozen mussels)
30 ml (2 tbsp) flour
500 ml (1 pint) milk
25 g (1 oz) chopped parsley
seasoning
50 g (2 oz) tasty Cheddar or Stilton cheese, grated
50 g (2 oz) fresh white breadcrumbs

To serve:
1 lemon, cut into wedges
chopped parsley
brown bread

1.   Preheat the oven to 200°C (400°F) mark 6.
2.   Melt the butter in a large pan, add the mushrooms and cook gently until softened. Add the mussels.
3.   Stir in the flour to form a roux, then gradually add the milk, stirring constantly.
4.   Bring the sauce to the boil and allow to simmer for 5 minutes. Add the parsley and seasoning.
5.   Divide the mixture between 6 individual large ramekin dishes or scallop shells.
6.   Mix the grated cheese and breadcrumbs together and sprinkle evenly over the tops of the dishes. Bake in the preheated oven for 15–20 minutes, until the top is crisp and golden.
7.   Serve while still bubbling, garnished with lemon wedges and chopped parsley, and accompanied by brown bread.

CEBICHE

NETHERWOOD HOTEL
Grange-over-Sands, Cumbria
Messrs J.D. & M.P. Fallowfield with chef Mr M. Fowler

.

A variety of seafood, cured in a lime or lemon juice marinade.

Serves 6

500 g (1 lb) mixed raw fish (e.g. prawns, scallops, haddock, plaice,
sole, etc.)
350 ml (14 fl oz) fresh lime or lemon juice
2 canned jalapeno chilli peppers, finely chopped
1 onion, roughly chopped
1 large tomato, skinned, seeded and chopped
90 ml (6 tbsp) olive oil
30 ml (2 tbsp) white wine vinegar
1.25 ml (¼ tsp) chopped oregano
5 ml (1 tsp) ground black pepper
salt

To serve:
lettuce
2 limes, cut into wedges
French bread

1. Clean, rinse and dry the fish thoroughly. Prepare the fish as
necessary, i.e. shell the scallops, peel and de-vein the prawns, skin the
large whole fish and cut into chunks.
2. Place all the prepared fish in a glass bowl, pour the lime juice over
the top, cover and leave to marinate for at least 4 hours, turning
occasionally with a wooden spoon. Drain off the juice.
3. In a separate bowl, mix together the chilli peppers, onion, tomato,
oil, vinegar, oregano and pepper with salt to taste. Add to the fish and
mix well. Refrigerate for 2–3 hours.
4. Let the fish stand at room temperature for 15 minutes before
serving, set on a bed of lettuce, garnished with lime wedges and
accompanied by fresh French bread.

MUSSEL & ONION SOUP

FOX & BARREL
Cotebrook, Cheshire

Alistair Appleton

.

This thick, hearty soup is a meal in its own right when served with quantities of piping hot garlic bread.

Serves 4

200 g (8 oz) butter or margarine
3 large onions, peeled and thinly sliced
50 g (2 oz) flour
1.5 litres (3 pints) good fish stock (see page 200)
25 g (1 oz) chopped parsley
seasoning
750 g (1½ lb) fresh mussels in their shells, cleaned
250 ml (10 fl oz) single cream

To serve:
chopped parsley

1. In a large saucepan, melt the butter and sweat the onions over a low heat until transparent.
2. Add the flour and stir to form a roux, cook for 2 minutes, then gradually add the fish stock, stirring constantly. Add parsley and season to taste.
3. Bring the soup to the boil, and allow it to simmer for 10 minutes, to thicken slightly and develop the flavour.
4. When you are almost ready to serve, add the mussels to the hot soup. Simmer for 1–2 minutes, stirring constantly, while the mussels open. Don't cook the mussels for any longer than this or they will toughen.
5. Stir the cream into the soup.
6. Ladle into warmed deep bowls and sprinkle with some extra chopped parsley.

NORTH SEA FISHERMAN'S SOUP

THE BRIDGE HOTEL
Ripon, North Yorkshire

Allan Reinhard with chef Kevin Warner

.

A delicious, creamy, fish and shellfish soup, flavoured with mushrooms and dill.

Serves 4–6

100 g (4 oz) butter
1 small onion, chopped
25 g (1 oz) mushrooms, chopped
50 g (2 oz) flour
1.5 litres (3 pints) good fish stock (see page 200)
100 g (4 oz) plaice fillets, skinned
100 g (4 oz) haddock fillets, skinned
100 g (4 oz) salmon, skinned
50 g (2 oz) cockles, shelled
50 g (2 oz) mussels, shelled
seasoning
125 ml (5 fl oz) single cream

To serve:
chopped fresh dill

1. Melt the butter in a large saucepan and fry the onion and mushrooms for 5 minutes until the onion has softened. Away from the heat, stir in the flour to form an even paste, then gradually add the fish stock, stirring constantly. Heat until the liquid begins to boil.
2. Cut the fish into chunks and add to the hot soup, together with the shellfish and seasoning. Bring to the boil and simmer for 15–20 minutes until the fish is cooked.
3. Stir in the cream, taste and correct seasoning.
4. Ladle into warmed bowls and sprinkle with chopped dill.

Note: The removed fish skins are ideal for preparing fish stock (see recipe on page 200).

VALE OF GLAMORGAN SOUP

OLD SWAN INN
Llantwit Major, South Glamorgan
Geoff & Myra Radford

.

Chicken and onion soup with crispy croûtons and melted cheese.

Serves 4–6

1 litre (2 pints) good, clear chicken stock (see page 201)
1 medium Spanish onion, finely chopped
1 medium leek, finely chopped
pinch of chopped dill
seasoning
100 ml (4 fl oz) oil
2 slices wholemeal bread, crusts removed and cut into
2 cm (¾ inch) dice
200 g (8 oz) Caerphilly cheese, grated
10 ml (2 tsp) snipped chives

1.   In a large saucepan, bring the stock to the boil and add the onion, leek, dill and seasoning. Cover and simmer for 30 minutes until the onion is soft.
2.   Heat the oil in another pan and fry the cubes of bread until golden. Drain thoroughly on kitchen paper.
3.   Divide the croûtons between individual serving bowls and sprinkle with the grated cheese. Pour the boiling hot soup over the cheese croûtons and sprinkle with the chives. Serve as soon as the cheese starts to melt.

CREAM OF COURGETTE & BONCHESTER CHEESE SOUP

THE OLD FORGE
Newmill on Teviot, Borders

Bill & Margaret Irving

.

A rich soup made from courgettes and the 'award winning' Bonchester cheese. If you are unable to buy Bonchester cheese, which is available through specialist cheese merchants, substitute with 90 g (3½ oz) ripe Brie.

Serves 4

25 g (1 oz) butter
1 medium onion, chopped
1 medium potato, peeled and diced
500 g (1 lb) courgettes, sliced
1.5 litres (3 pints) good chicken stock (see page 201)
1 small Bonchester cheese
salt
ground white pepper

To serve:
double cream
chopped fresh chervil

1. Melt the butter in a large saucepan and use to fry the onion until soft but not coloured.
2. Stir in the potato and courgettes, cook for 1 minute and then add the stock. Bring to the boil and simmer for 15 minutes, or until the potato is soft.
3. Dice the cheese and blend, together with the soup, in the liquidiser. Return the soup to the pan and reheat to just below boiling point. Taste and season as necessary.
4. Serve, topped with a swirl of cream and a sprinkling of chopped fresh chervil.

LEEK & CORIANDER SOUP

LONG'S RESTAURANT
Truro, Cornwall

Ian & Ann Long

.

Creamed leek and onion soup, flavoured with ground coriander.

Serves 8

200 g (8 oz) onions
1 kg (2 lb) leeks, washed
100 g (4 oz) butter
30 ml (2 tbsp) ground coriander seeds
250 ml (10 fl oz) medium dry sherry
1.5 litres (3 pints) good chicken stock (see page 201)
5 ml (1 tsp) honey
seasoning

To serve:
coriander leaves
fresh bread

1.   Slice the onions and leeks into pieces approximately the same size to ensure even cooking.
2.   Melt the butter in a large saucepan, add the onions and cook until transparent. Stir in the leeks, coriander and sherry.
3.   Reduce the heat to the lowest possible level, cover the vegetables with a sheet of greaseproof paper and put a lid on the saucepan. Cook for 40–45 minutes until the vegetables are tender.
4.   Away from the heat, remove the greaseproof and pour in the stock. Liquidise the soup until smooth, then pass the resulting liquid through a fine sieve. It may be necessary to purée the soup in several batches. Taste, add the honey and seasoning.
5.   Heat through thoroughly, garnish with a few fresh coriander leaves and serve with fresh bread.

PEA, APPLE & HAZELNUT SOUP

LONG'S RESTAURANT
Truro, Cornwall

Ian & Ann Long

.

A sweet, fresh-tasting, pea soup. As an alternative, cook a little mint
with the peas, omit the hazelnuts and garnish with sliced lemon.

Serves 8

500 g (1 lb) eating apples
100 g (4 oz) butter
200 g (8 oz) onions, finely chopped
1 kg (2 lb) fresh or frozen peas
¼ of a nutmeg, grated
250 ml (10 fl oz) dry sherry
1.5 litres (3 pints) good chicken stock (see page 201)
seasoning
caster sugar

To serve:
double cream
30 ml (2 tbsp) ground hazelnuts
brown bread

1.   Do not peel, but core and slice the apples.
2.   Melt the butter in a large saucepan, add the onions and cook until
transparent.
3.   Add the apples, peas, nutmeg and sherry to the pan. Reduce the
heat to as low a setting as possible, cover with a circle of greaseproof
paper, put a lid on the pan and cook for 30 minutes until the apples
and peas are tender.
4.   Away from the heat, remove the greaseproof and pour in the
stock. Liquidise the soup until smooth and pass the resulting liquid
through a fine sieve. It may be necessary to purée and sieve the soup
in several batches. Taste and season with salt, pepper and sugar as
necessary.
5.   Reheat, then serve swirled with cream and sprinkled with ground
hazelnuts, accompanied by brown bread.

CHEESE & CIDER SOUP

THE STEPPES COUNTRY HOUSE HOTEL
Ullingswick, Herefordshire

Henry & Tricia Howland

.

A thick, creamy, chilled cheese soup. Serve as a starter or with crusty French bread for lunch or supper.

Serves 6–8

600 ml (1¼ pints) milk
1 onion, roughly chopped
3 cloves
3 bay leaves
350 g (14 oz) strong Cheddar cheese, grated
750 ml (1½ pints) dry cider
3 egg yolks
125 ml (5 fl oz) single cream
seasoning

To serve:
15 ml (1 tbsp) snipped chives
5 ml (1 tsp) paprika

1. In a pan, bring to the boil the milk, onion, cloves and bay leaves. Turn off the heat and allow to infuse for 15 minutes.
2. In another pan, mix together the grated cheese and cider. Gently heat together until the cheese melts.
3. Remove the onion, cloves and bay leaf from the milk.
4. Using a food processor or whisk, mix together the liquid cheese, milk, egg yolks and cream until thoroughly blended. Heat this mixture for 10 minutes, stirring constantly until it thickens. Taste and adjust seasoning.
5. Refrigerate for at least 3 hours before serving, garnished with chives and a dash of paprika.

MAIN COURSES

SIRLOIN STEAK LORD CHANDOS

PENGETHLEY MANOR HOTEL
Ross on Wye, Herefordshire

Patrick & Geraldine Wisker with chef Ferdinand Van Der Knaap

.

Sirloin steaks filled with a mix of apples and Stilton, coated in mustard and rolled oats, fried in butter. Serve with garden peas, sauté potatoes and a sauce of puréed apples.

Serves 6

150 g (6 oz) Stilton cheese, crumbled
2 eating apples, peeled and diced
100 g (4 oz) butter, softened
6 × 200 g (8 oz) thick-cut sirloin steaks
seasoning
10 ml (2 tsp) dry English mustard
50 g (2 oz) flour
2 eggs, lightly beaten
100 g (4 oz) rolled oats

To serve:
1 bunch of watercress
lemon slices

1.   In a bowl, mix together the Stilton, apples and half the butter.
2.   Using a thin-bladed knife, cut a horizontal pocket in the side of each steak, keeping the opening as small as possible and taking care not to cut through the meat. Swing the knife around inside the steak to widen the pocket, fill with the Stilton stuffing and press the opening edges together.
3.   Season and sprinkle the mustard over the steaks. Dust the steaks with flour, dip in the egg and finally press into the oats to coat evenly.
4.   Melt the remaining butter in a large frying pan and gently fry the steaks for 10–15 minutes, according to taste. Serve immediately, garnished with sprigs of watercress and slices of lemon.

GINGER BEEF TUB

THE TATTLER
Edinburgh, Lothian

Mr & Mrs Thomson with chef Bobby Clarke

.

An aromatic ginger and beef casserole. Serve with saffron rice or jacket potatoes.

Serves 4–6

15 ml (1 tbsp) oil
750 g (1½ lb) lean silverside beef, sliced into strips
1 large onion, diced
5 ml (1 tsp) mixed herbs
2.5 cm (1 inch) fresh root ginger, grated
3 cloves garlic, crushed
1 green chilli, chopped
3 bay leaves
20 ml (4 tsp) tomato purée
seasoning
45 ml (3 tbsp) flour
750 ml (1½ pints) good beef stock (see page 200)
20 ml (4 tsp) redcurrant jelly
75 g (3 oz) mixed red and green peppers, sliced
125 ml (5 fl oz) single cream
300 g (12 oz) tomatoes, peeled and diced
50 ml (2 fl oz) ginger wine

1.   Preheat the oven to 220°C (425°F) mark 7.
2.   Heat the oil in a large saucepan or flameproof casserole dish. Fry the beef until sealed and brown on all sides.
3.   Add the onion, herbs, ginger, garlic, chilli, bay leaves, tomato purée and seasoning, stir and cook for several minutes.
4.   Stir in the flour and cook for a further 5 minutes, then blend in the stock, bring to the boil and add the redcurrant jelly.
5.   If using a saucepan, transfer the stew to a casserole dish now. Cover and cook in the hot oven for 1¼ hours or until the meat is tender.
6.   Stir in the peppers, cream, tomatoes and ginger wine. Cover and return to the oven for 10 minutes. Taste and correct seasoning.
7.   Ladle into warmed deep plates or large bowls and serve.

HOME-SPICED TOPSIDE OF BEEF

LONG'S RESTAURANT
Truro, Cornwall

Ian & Ann Long

.

Marinated topside flavoured with brandy and roasted slowly on a bed of root vegetables and wine. Serve with red cabbage, cauliflower in parsley sauce and roast potatoes. Whenever possible, allow the beef to marinate for 5 days. If you have one, use a fish kettle to marinate and braise the meat. Alternatively, marinate in a china or glass mixing bowl, although you may have to cut the meat in half and marinate it in 2 separate bowls.

Serves 8

2.5 kg (5 lb) topside of beef, rolled into a long thin (almost sausage) shape, tied at 2.5 cm (1 inch) intervals

For the marinade:
2 litres (4 pints) water
300 g (12 oz) sea salt
200 g (8 oz) brown sugar
15 g (½ oz) saltpetre
1 bay leaf
15 ml (1 tbsp) dried thyme
6 peppercorns

For cooking the beef:
200 g (8 oz) pork rind
2 carrots, sliced
2 sticks celery, sliced
2 onions, sliced with skins left on
1 litre (2 pints) red wine
125 ml (5 fl oz) brandy
5 ml (1 tsp) dried marjoram

To serve:
500 ml (1 pint) brown sauce (see page 203)
seasoning

1.   First prepare the marinade. Bring the water to the boil in a large saucepan and add all the other marinade ingredients, stirring until the salt and sugar have dissolved. Pour into a large container and allow to cool completely.

2.   Place the beef in a fish kettle or mixing bowl and pour the liquid over the top. Cover with a double layer of greaseproof paper and partly cover with a lid.

3.   Leave the meat to marinate in a cool dark place for 3–5 days, turning twice a day, where possible at equal intervals, e.g. at 8 a.m. and 8 p.m.

4.   To cook the meat, preheat the oven to 180°C (350°F) mark 4.

5.   Remove the beef from the marinade, wipe the meat dry and throw away the marinade liquid.

6.   Cut the pork rind into thin strips. Lay half the rind on the base of the roasting tin or fish kettle and place the beef on top. Arrange the vegetables around the meat, then cook, uncovered, in the hot oven for 20 minutes.

7.   While the meat is cooking, heat together the wine and brandy.

8.   Remove the meat from the oven and lower the temperature to 140°C (275°F) mark 1.

9.   Pour the hot wine and brandy around the meat and sprinkle with the marjoram. Cover the meat with the remaining pork rind, a double layer of greaseproof paper and completely seal with foil. Cook in the lowest part of the oven for 2½ hours, check, baste and return the meat to the oven for another 15 minutes.

10.   Remove the meat from the pan and leave to rest for 15 minutes, then wrap in foil to keep warm.

11.   Skim off any fat that has formed on the top of the cooking liquid, then strain the remaining juices into a saucepan. Whisk in the brown sauce, taste and season.

12.   Remove the string from the beef, carve a few slices off the joint and arrange on a serving platter. Pour a couple of spoons of sauce over the meat to make it shine before serving, offering the rest of the gravy in a warm jug or sauce boat.

OLD-FASHIONED STEAK & KIDNEY PUDDING

THE TEMPLE HOTEL
Matlock Bath, Derbyshire

Seigfried & Gertrude Esst

.

A traditional steamed steak and kidney pudding. Serve with Brussels sprouts and buttered boiled potatoes.

Serves 4

100 g (4 oz) ox kidney
750 g (1½ lb) lean stewing steak, cubed
30 ml (2 tbsp) flour
seasoning
30 ml (2 tbsp) oil
2 onions, peeled and sliced
100 g (4 oz) mushrooms, sliced
3 bay leaves
1 litre (2 pints) good beef stock (see page 200)

For the suet crust:
200 g (8 oz) self raising flour
2.5 ml (½ tsp) salt
100 g (4 oz) suet
125 ml (5 fl oz) cold water

1.   Trim any gristle from the kidney and cut into 1.25 cm (½ inch) dice. Mix the steak and kidney together in a bowl and toss in the flour and seasoning to coat the meat lightly.
2.   Heat the oil in a saucepan and gently cook the onions until transparent. Add the steak and kidney and continue to cook until the meat is sealed. Add the mushrooms, bay leaves and stock and bring to the boil. Simmer for 15–20 minutes, stirring occasionally, then turn off the heat and allow the pudding filling to cool.
3.   Meanwhile prepare the suet crust. Sift the flour and salt together into a bowl. Add the suet and mix. Using a round-ended knife, stir in enough of the water to form a light, elastic dough.
4.   Turn the dough out onto a lightly floured surface and knead to shape into a ball. Cover and leave to rest for 15 minutes.
5.   Grease a 1 litre (2 pint) pudding basin. Reserve a quarter of the prepared crust for the pudding lid and roll out the remaining pastry, on a lightly floured surface, to form a circle 5 cm (2 inches) wider than the top of the basin, about 0.5 cm (¼ inch) thick.

6.   Sprinkle the pastry with flour, fold in half, then in half again to form a triangle. Lower the pastry into the prepared basin, point first, and carefully mould into the sides.

7.   Spoon the cooled prepared filling into the lined basin, turn the overhanging pastry sides over the filling and brush the pastry edge with water. Roll out the remaining pastry to form a circle to fit the top of the basin and place over the filling, pressing the pastry edges together to form a tight seal.

8.   Tie a double thickness of buttered greaseproof paper or foil over the top of the pudding, secured with string around the outside of the basin (there must be room for the pudding to expand during cooking so, if necessary, make a tuck in the covering material). Tie a clean tea towel around the top of the pudding, then tie over the dish to form a 'handle' for the basin. It is important that the coverings are secure to prevent water getting into the basin during cooking.

9.   Place a heatproof plate in the base of a large saucepan, position the pudding on top and pour enough boiling water into the pan to come halfway up the sides of the basin. Steam the pudding briskly for 3½ hours, topping up the water level as necessary.

10.   Leave the pudding to stand for 10 minutes before removing the cloth and paper and turning out onto a deep serving dish.

SCOTTISH ROAST BEEF

MILTON OF GOLLANFIELD
Inverness, Highland

Lilias E. MacBean

.

Buy sirloin, topside or silverside joints of Scottish beef for a really succulent roast. Allow 200–300 g (8–12 oz) per person if buying meat on the bone, 150–200 g (6–8 oz) per person for a boned joint.

Calculate the roasting time for boned joints by allowing 20 minutes per 500 g (1 lb) and adding 20 minutes to the total cooking time for rare meat, 40 minutes for a well done joint. Cook at 220°C (425°F) mark 7. For meat on the bone, allow 25 minutes per 500 g (1 lb) cooking time, plus 20–40 minutes according to taste.

Rub salt into the fat surrounding the joint and place 50 g (2 oz) of dripping on top. Roast uncovered in a preheated oven and baste several times during cooking.

Once cooked, wrap the joint in foil and leave to stand for 20 minutes before carving so that the meat absorbs most of its juices.

Serve wafer thin slices of meat with gravy, horseradish sauce, mustard, roast potatoes and seasonal vegetables.

AYTON HALL BEEF

AYTON HALL
Low Green, North Yorkshire
Melvin R. Rhodes

.

Fillet of beef, cooked whole for maximum flavour, served in a rich beer sauce. Serve with steamed broccoli florets and creamed potatoes.

Serves 4

1 litre (2 pints) good beef stock (see page 200)
750 g (1½ lb) fillet of beef, trimmed
oil for brushing
seasoning
pinch of ground mace
pinch of celery salt
pinch of grated nutmeg
250 ml (10 fl oz) stout
50 g (2 oz) butter

To serve:
pinch of grated nutmeg
1 bunch watercress

1.   In a large saucepan, bring the beef stock to the boil and simmer until reduced to 250 ml (10 fl oz). Preheat the oven or grill.
2.   Brush the meat with oil and dust with seasoning, ground mace, celery salt and grated nutmeg.
3.   Heat a frying pan, add the meat and cook for several minutes on all sides, leaving the meat just underdone for your taste. Transfer the meat to a roasting tin, cover and keep warm in the hot oven or grill.
4.   Pour the reduced stock into the frying pan and bring to the boil, stirring to take up the meat juices from the pan. As the stock begins to thicken, add the beer and continue to simmer.
5.   Remove the meat from the oven or grill, carve into 16 to 20 slices, cover once more and return to the grill to keep warm. Add to the sauce any juices that have come out of the meat during carving.
6.   Away from the heat, whisk small knobs of butter into the sauce, until it becomes rich and shiny. Strain, taste and correct seasoning.
7.   Flood individual warm serving plates with sauce, arrange 4–5 slices of beef in a fan on each plate. Sprinkle a little nutmeg over the meat, garnish with watercress and serve.

*Spinach & Mushroom Timbales with Herb &
Sour Cream Sauce (page 22)*

NORMANTON'S OWN BEEF RUTLAND

NORMANTON PARK HOTEL
Rutland Water, Leicestershire
Mr & Mrs A.F. Chamberlain

Medallions of beef fillet, cooked with bacon, onions and mushrooms in a cream, red wine and Rutland cheese sauce. Serve with green beans and creamed potatoes.

Serves 6

1 kg (2 lb) beef fillet
oil for brushing
100 g (4 oz) butter
150 g (6 oz) lean bacon, diced
1 medium onion, finely chopped
150 g (6 oz) mushrooms, sliced
125 ml (5 fl oz) red wine
250 ml (10 fl oz) double cream
50 g (2 oz) Rutland cheese, grated (as an alternative, use Cheddar cheese)

To serve:
chopped parsley

1.   Preheat the oven or grill to a moderate temperature.
2.   Trim the fillet as necessary and cut into 24 slices.
3.   Brush with oil, then heat a heavy-based frying pan on the hob. Quickly seal the meat on both sides, reduce the heat and continue to cook until the beef is just underdone for your taste. Remove from the pan, place on an ovenproof dish, cover and keep warm.
4.   Add the butter, bacon, onion and mushrooms to the pan and fry for 10 minutes until the bacon turns golden and the onion transparent. Add the red wine, bring to the boil and allow to simmer for 5 minutes.
5.   Pour in the cream, and stir until the sauce thickens to a coating consistency. Sprinkle in the cheese, taste and correct seasoning.
6.   Arrange the meat on a serving dish and whisk any juices that have collected on the storage plate into the sauce. Spoon a little sauce over the meat, garnish with parsley and serve immediately.

Eastern Sole Fillets (page 42)

CALVES' LIVER WITH ORANGE GLAZE

RUDLOE PARK HOTEL
Corsham, Wiltshire

Mr I.C. Overend with chef Geoff Bell

Wafer thin slices of calves' liver, lightly fried in butter, with a tangy orange and Grand Marnier sauce. Serve with a selection of fresh vegetables or salad.

Serves 4

2 oranges
4 × 150 g (6 oz) thin slices calves' liver
seasoning
flour for dusting
50 g (2 oz) butter
200 ml (8 fl oz) white wine
5 ml (1 tsp) white wine vinegar
5 ml (1 tsp) light brown sugar
45 ml (3 tbsp) Grand Marnier
45 ml (3 tbsp) reduced chicken stock (see page 201)

1.   First prepare the oranges by grating the zest from 1 orange. Then, cut peel and pith from both oranges. Hold the oranges over a bowl (to catch the juice) and cut the individual segments away from the central orange filaments.
2.   Wash and pat the liver dry with kitchen paper. Sprinkle with seasoning and flour, shaking off any excess.
3.   Melt the butter in a frying pan and, when it is hot, cook the coated liver for 20–30 seconds on each side, until it has turned a golden brown.
4.   Remove the liver from the pan and place on a warmed serving plate. Cover and keep at the bottom of a warm oven while you prepare the sauce.
5.   Add the white wine to the remaining butter and liver juices in the pan and simmer until reduced to half volume. Stir in the vinegar, sugar, and grated orange zest and continue cooking for 30 seconds.
6.   Pour in the Grand Marnier and flame, then add the chicken stock, orange segments and their juice (the addition of these liquids will put out the flames). Continue to simmer the sauce for 1 minute, taste and correct seasoning.

7. Remove the liver from the oven, pour the sauce over the meat and serve immediately.

Note: This quick cooking time is only appropriate for use with very thinly sliced pieces of liver; if using thicker slices increase the cooking time accordingly.

LE GRANDGOUSIER'S VEAL

LE GRANDGOUSIER
Brighton, Sussex

Mr L.M. Harris with chef Mr O.P. Godfrey

Veal escalopes in a cream, mustard and sherry sauce with white grapes and croûtons. Serve with a light salad and rice or noodles.

Serves 4

125 ml (5 fl oz) sweet sherry
500 ml (1 pint) double cream
15 ml (1 tbsp) English mustard
2 thin slices bread, crusts removed
50 g (2 oz) butter
4 × 150 g (6 oz) veal escalopes
200 g (8 oz) seedless grapes

1. In a bowl, mix together the sherry, cream and mustard.
2. Prepare the croûtons. Cut the bread diagonally into quarters to form triangles. Melt the butter in a large frying pan and quickly fry the bread until golden on both sides. Remove from the pan, drain on kitchen paper and keep warm.
3. In the butter left in the frying pan, fry the escalopes for 2 minutes on both sides until sealed and just turning brown. Add the sherry mixture to the pan and bring to the boil. Add the grapes, reduce the heat and allow to simmer until the liquid has thickened slightly.
4. Arrange the veal on a serving plate, spoon sauce over the top, garnish with the croûtons and serve immediately.

ESCALOPES OF VEAL HARRIET

PENGETHLEY MANOR HOTEL
Ross on Wye, Herefordshire

*Patrick & Geraldine Wisker with
chef Ferdinand Van Der Knaap*

.

Veal escalopes, rolled around a sauce of ham, cheese and mushrooms, coated in breadcrumbs and gently fried in butter. Serve with a light gravy, green beans and creamed potatoes.

Serves 4

4 × 125 g (5 oz) veal escalopes
65 g (2½ oz) butter
15 g (½ oz) flour
150 ml (6 fl oz) milk
50 g (2 oz) Cheddar cheese, grated
50 g (2 oz) 'off the bone' ham, finely diced
50 g (2 oz) mushrooms, finely diced
seasoning
flour for dusting
1 egg, lightly beaten
150 g (6 oz) breadcrumbs

To serve:
lemon wedges
watercress
chopped parsley

1.   Lay the veal between 2 sheets of greaseproof paper and beat with a meat mallet or rolling pin until wafer thin.
2.   Melt 15 g (½ oz) of the butter in a saucepan, stir in the flour then gradually add the milk to form a white sauce. Stir in the grated cheese and continue to heat until the cheese has melted. Add the ham and mushrooms and season to taste, then allow to cool slightly.
3.   Place a spoonful of the cheese and ham mixture at one end of each escalope, then roll up, making sure the filling doesn't protrude at either end.
4.   Dust the veal rolls in flour, then the beaten egg and finally coat in breadcrumbs. Repeat the coating process until you have a reasonable thickness of crumbs around the veal. Cover and refrigerate the coated veal for 15 minutes.

5. Melt the remaining butter in a large frying pan and fry the veal over a gentle heat, turning constantly, for 8–10 minutes, until the breadcrumbs are golden and the veal rolls are cooked through.
6. Arrange on a warmed serving dish and garnish with lemon wedges, watercress and chopped parsley.

WINTER VEAL

THE REDFERN HOTEL
Cleobury Mortimer, Worcestershire

Mr & Mrs J. Redfern

.

Veal escalopes in a creamy, ginger sauce. Serve with a crisp fennel or carrot salad and noodles.

Serves 4

4 × 150 g (6 oz) veal escalopes
seasoning
flour for dusting
50 g (2 oz) butter
90 ml (6 tbsp) ginger wine
60 ml (4 tbsp) single cream
juice of ½ lemon

To serve:
1 lemon, sliced
1 small bunch parsley

1. Place the escalopes between 2 sheets of greaseproof paper and beat until thin with a meat mallet or rolling pin. Season and dust with flour.
2. Melt the butter in a large frying pan and, when very hot, add the veal (cook the veal in several batches if necessary). Fry the escalopes briskly on both sides for 5–6 minutes until browned, then lift the slices onto a warmed serving plate, cover and keep warm in the oven while preparing the sauce.
3. Add the ginger wine to the pan, bring to the boil and simmer for 1 minute, stirring, to take up all the meat juices from the pan. Add the cream, lemon juice and seasoning. Stir until warmed through and slightly thickened.
4. Pour the sauce over the escalopes and serve immediately, garnished with lemon slices and parsley.

ROSETTES OF LAMB DANIEL PATRICK

GREEN LAWNS HOTEL
Falmouth, Cornwall
Robert Collings with chef Patrick Quinn

.

Nuggets of spring lamb, fried in garlic, surrounded by a rich port gravy and served with a honey and mint mayonnaise. This recipe is designed to be served with each portion of lamb sitting on a minted potato cake (recipe on page 147), producing a wonderful flavour combination. Serve with lightly steamed fresh asparagus spears and courgette sticks. For ease of preparation, ask the butcher to bone and trim the loin of lamb for you, or buy ready-prepared noisettes.

Serves 4

For the mayonnaise:
5 ml (1 tsp) runny honey
5 ml (1 tsp) chopped mint leaves
125 ml (5 fl oz) mayonnaise
seasoning

For the lamb:
1 kg (2 lb) loin of lamb, boned and trimmed
seasoning
1 clove garlic
50 g (2 oz) butter
10 ml (2 tsp) flour
100 ml (4 fl oz) port
10 ml (2 tsp) redcurrant jelly
100 ml (4 fl oz) water

To serve:
1 quantity of minted potato cakes (see page 147)
sprigs of fresh mint
4 small bunches of redcurrants

1.   First prepare the mayonnaise dressing. Stir the honey and mint into the mayonnaise, season to taste, cover and refrigerate until required.
2.   Cut the loin of lamb into 16 pieces and lightly season the meat.
3.   Rub the clove of garlic over the surface of a frying pan, then melt

the butter in the pan. Fry the lamb in melted butter for 5–8 minutes until cooked to your liking, remove and place on a heated dish, cover and keep warm.

4. Stir the flour into the butter left in the pan, then add the port, half the redcurrant jelly and the water, scraping all the meat juices from the base of the pan as you bring the gravy to the boil. Simmer for 2 minutes and season to taste.

5. Spread the remaining redcurrant jelly over the hot minted potato cakes and arrange the lamb on top. Flood the plate with the gravy, garnish with fresh mint and bunches of redcurrants. Serve with the chilled mayonnaise dressing.

LAMB CHOPS CAERPHILLY

OLD SWAN INN
Llantwit Major, South Glamorgan
Geoff & Myra Radford

.

Lamb chops, coated with herbs, with a Caerphilly cheese sauce. Serve with lightly boiled leeks, broccoli florets and minted new potatoes.

Serves 4

8 large or 12 small lamb chops
10 ml (2 tsp) olive oil
10 ml (2 tsp) chopped marjoram
10 ml (2 tsp) chopped rosemary
seasoning
125 ml (5 fl oz) double cream
25 g (1 oz) butter
150 g (6 oz) Caerphilly cheese, grated

To serve:
snipped chives or chopped parsley

1. Brush the lamb with oil and press the herbs and seasoning into the meat, to form a complete herb coating.

2. Heat the grill and cook the lamb, turning carefully until done to your taste.

3. While the lamb is cooking, heat together the cream and butter, add the cheese and stir until the cheese has melted. Season to taste.

4. Arrange the lamb chops on a warmed serving dish, spoon a little sauce over the top, garnish and serve immediately.

GHILLIES HOT POT

GREEN PARK HOTEL
Pitlochry, Perthshire

Mr & Mrs G.C. Brown

Individual lamb and vegetable pies. Serve with braised courgettes and jacket potatoes.

Serves 6

2 large onions, diced
30 ml (2 tbsp) oil
1.25 kg (2½ lb) lean shoulder of lamb, diced into 2.5 cm (1 inch) cubes
flour for dusting
500 ml (1 pint) stock
1 small turnip, peeled and diced
1 medium carrot, peeled and diced
1 small leek, washed and sliced
200 g (8 oz) button mushrooms
200 g (8 oz) tomatoes, peeled and seeded
1 bay leaf
5 ml (1 tsp) mixed spice
5 ml (1 tsp) chopped fresh rosemary
seasoning
500 g (1 lb) puff pastry
milk to glaze

1. Preheat the oven to 180°C (350°F) mark 4.
2. In a flameproof casserole dish, fry the onions in the oil until transparent.
3. Toss the diced lamb in the flour to coat. Add to the casserole and cook, stirring constantly, until the meat is sealed and browned.
4. Stir in the stock, turnip, carrot, leek, mushroom, tomatoes, bay leaf, spice, rosemary and seasoning. Cover and braise in the hot oven for 1½ hours until the meat is tender.
5. Leave the stew to cool, then spoon into 6 individual pie dishes.
6. On a lightly floured surface, roll out the pastry and use to cover the pies. Moisten the edge of each dish before covering to form a good seal. Decorate the top of each pie with pastry trimmings and brush with a little milk.
7. Refrigerate for at least 30 minutes to let the pastry rest before baking.
8. Bake at the centre of the oven at 230°C (450°F) mark 8 for 25–30 minutes until the pastry is crisp and golden.

LOMO DE CERDO ALBERGUE

LA GIRALDA
Pinner, Middlesex

David Brown

.

Pork cutlets filled with mild goat's cheese and topped with a mustard sauce. Serve with plain steamed vegetables, salad and rice.

Serves 6

6 lean pork cutlets
seasoning
300 g (12 oz) mild goat's cheese
25 g (1 oz) butter

For the sauce:
250 ml (10 fl oz) milk
2 bay leaves
sprig of thyme
½ small onion
pinch of grated nutmeg
25 g (1 oz) butter
15 g (½ oz) flour
30 ml (2 tbsp) double cream
25 g (1 oz) Dijon mustard
seasoning

1.   First prepare the sauce. Put the milk, bay leaves, thyme, onion and nutmeg into a pan together. Slowly bring to the boil. Remove from the heat and leave to infuse for 15 minutes, then strain.
2.   In a separate pan, melt the butter, stir in the flour to form a roux and cook for 2 minutes until sandy in texture. Slowly add the strained milk, stirring constantly to form a smooth sauce, bring to the boil and allow to simmer for 3 minutes until the sauce has thickened. Stir in the cream and mustard, taste and adjust seasoning.
3.   Preheat the oven to 180°C (350°F) mark 4.
4.   Trim most of the fat from the pork and remove the bones. Slice the pork open through the middle, leaving the meat joined at one side, and open out like the wings of a butterfly. Sprinkle with seasoning.
5.   Place 50 g (2 oz) goat's cheese in the centre of each cutlet and fold the meat back together to its original shape, enclosing the cheese.
6.   Melt the butter in a large frying pan and gently cook the chops for 3 minutes on each side. Arrange the cutlets in an ovenproof dish and pour the sauce over the top. Cover and bake in the preheated oven for 10–15 minutes, until the sauce has turned golden brown.

FILLET OF PORK ORIENTAL

FASGANEOIN HOTEL
Pitlochry, Tayside

The Turk Family

.

Roasted pork fillet, sliced and served with a spicy, fruity sauce and rings of lightly sautéed pineapple. Serve with a crisp salad and buttered rice or noodles.

Serves 4

45 ml (3 tbsp) oil
500 g (1 lb) pork fillets (trimmed weight)
seasoning
5 ml (1 tsp) mixed spice
1 Spanish onion, diced
1 clove garlic, crushed
5 ml (1 tsp) hot curry powder
1 × 397 g (14 oz) can of pineapple in fruit juice (8 rings)
100 ml (4 fl oz) chicken stock
15 ml (1 tbsp) Worcestershire Sauce
15 ml (1 tbsp) mild chilli sauce
30 ml (2 tbsp) tomato purée
30 ml (2 tbsp) soy sauce
5 ml (1 tsp) salt
2 pieces preserved stem ginger, cut into thin strips
5 ml (1 tsp) dried mixed herbs
5 ml (1 tsp) cornflour
25 g (1 oz) butter
250 ml (10 fl oz) single cream

1. Preheat the oven to 220°C (425°F) mark 7.
2. Brush a little of the oil over the pork fillets, then sprinkle with seasoning and mixed spice. Heat the remaining oil in a frying pan and use to fry the fillets until golden brown on all sides. Keep the cooking oil and pork juices to prepare the sauce.
3. Tightly wrap the fillets in foil and place on a baking tray in the hot oven for 20 minutes until the sauce is prepared.
4. Fry the onion and garlic in the reserved oil. Add the curry powder, juice of the tin of pineapple slices, stock, Worcestershire Sauce, chilli sauce, tomato purée, soy sauce, salt, stem ginger and herbs, stir and bring to the boil. Allow to simmer for 2 minutes.
5. Mix the cornflour to a smooth paste with a little cold water, stir

into the sauce and continue to cook, stirring constantly until the sauce has thickened slightly, approximately 2 minutes. Taste and adjust the seasoning.

6.   Melt the butter in a frying pan and gently fry the pineapple rings until they are golden at the edges and warmed through.

7.   Remove the pork from the oven and cut into thin slices. Reheat the sauce if necessary, then away from the heat stir in the cream. Arrange the food on a warm serving platter, alternating slices of pineapple and pork down the centre. Pour a little sauce over the dish, and serve the remainder in a sauce jug.

HONEY ROASTED HAM

WOODLAND DELL HOTEL
Lynton, North Devon

Verna & Malcolm Holt

.

Gammon baked with honey and fresh pineapple. Serve with fresh sugar peas, sweetcorn and sauté potatoes.

Serves 4

1.5 kg (3 lb) gammon joint
either 1 fresh pineapple
or 250 ml (10 fl oz) canned pineapple in its own juice
75 g (3 oz) honey
2 tomatoes

1.   Soak the gammon in cold water overnight to remove excess salt.

2.   In a saucepan, cover the gammon with fresh cold water, bring to the boil and simmer for 30 minutes.

3.   Preheat the oven to 220°C (425°F) mark 7.

4.   Drain the meat and pat dry with kitchen paper. Place in a roasting tin and bake in the preheated oven for 1 hour.

5.   Liquidise some of the pineapple until you have 250 ml (10 fl oz) of liquid and mix with the honey. Pour this mixture over the ham, return to the oven and continue baking for a further 20 minutes.

6.   Slice and peel the remaining pineapple to give 4 rings.

7.   Cut the gammon into 4 slices, top each slice with a pineapple ring and half a tomato. Serve immediately.

HEREFORDSHIRE GAMMON

THE STEPPES COUNTRY HOUSE HOTEL
Ullingswick, Herefordshire

Henry & Tricia Howland

.

Pastry-wrapped gammon steaks, served with a cider sauce. Serve with braised celery (see page 151), creamed spinach and potato casserole (see page 148).

Serves 6

6 gammon steaks
50 g (2 oz) sultanas
seasoning
500–750 g (1–1½ lb) puff pastry
1 egg, lightly beaten
1 dessert apple
30 ml (2 tbsp) lemon juice

For the sauce:
250 ml (10 fl oz) good chicken stock (see page 201)
25 g (1 oz) flour
350 ml (14 fl oz) dry cider
3 bay leaves
3 cloves
seasoning

1.   Preheat the oven to 220°C (425°F) mark 7.
2.   Top each gammon steak with a few sultanas and season.
3.   On a lightly floured surface, roll out the pastry until very thin. Cut into 2.5 cm (1 inch) wide, long strips. Individually wrap each steak in the pastry strips, binding it over and over like a bandage until the gammon is completely enclosed. Seal the edges by brushing with beaten egg.
4.   Arrange the parcels on a baking sheet, brush with egg and bake at the top of the hot oven for 20 minutes until well risen and golden brown, then cover with foil or buttered paper and continue to cook for a further 20 minutes.
5.   Slice the apple and sprinkle with the lemon juice.
6.   Prepare the cider sauce. In a small pan, gradually mix the stock into the flour to form a smooth paste. Add the cider, bay leaves, cloves and seasoning. Gently heat, stirring, until the sauce has thickened. Sieve to remove the bay leaves and cloves before serving.
7.   Serve the gammon steaks, topped with the apple slices and accompanied by the hot sauce.

LEEK & BACON GRATIN

BRENTWOOD HOTEL
Rotherham, Yorkshire

James Lister

.

Leeks, wrapped in bacon and served in a cheese sauce. Serve with salad and fresh hunks of granary bread. For a change, wrap the leeks in half a slice of ham spread with mustard instead of the bacon.

Serves 6

4 large leeks
6 rashers rindless bacon
40 g (1½ oz) butter
25 g (1 oz) flour
500 ml (1 pint) milk
1 egg yolk
seasoning
pinch of grated nutmeg
15 ml (1 tbsp) chopped parsley
200 g (8 oz) Cheddar cheese, grated

1. Cut each leek into 3 pieces. Cook in boiling salted water until just tender, then drain.
2. Halve the rashers of bacon and grill until just browned.
3. Wrap a rasher of bacon around each leek and pack tightly into an ovenproof dish.
4. Preheat the oven to 150°C (300°F) mark 2.
5. Prepare the cheese sauce. Melt the butter in a saucepan, stir in the flour to form a roux and cook for 2 minutes until sandy in texture. Gradually stir in the milk to form a smooth sauce, then add the egg yolk, seasoning, nutmeg, parsley and half the cheese. Pour over the leeks.
6. Sprinkle the remaining cheese over the top of the dish and bake in the preheated oven for 20–25 minutes until the sauce is bubbling and the cheese topping crunchy.

ROSE & CROWN FAGGOTS

ROSE & CROWN INN
Nympsfield, Gloucestershire

Bob & Linda Woodman

•

Traditional West Country faggots in a rich gravy. Serve with fresh vegetables and jacket potatoes.

Serves 4

500 g (1 lb) pig's liver
2 large onions, chopped
75 g (3 oz) shredded suet
100 g (4 oz) breadcrumbs
5 ml (1 tsp) chopped sage
seasoning
4 rashers bacon
250 ml (10 fl oz) boiling water
either gravy browning powder to taste
or 500 ml (1 pint) brown sauce (see page 203)

To serve:
chopped parsley

1.   Preheat the oven to 180°C (350°F) mark 4.
2.   Mince the liver and onions together into a large bowl, or rough chop in the food processor. Add the suet, breadcrumbs, sage and seasoning. Mix all the ingredients together thoroughly, using clean hands.
3.   Cut the bacon rashers in half. Divide the faggot mixture into 8 equal portions and, using the palm of the hand, roll each portion into a ball. Wrap a half rasher of bacon around each faggot, then pack into a casserole dish. Pour the boiling water over the faggots, cover and bake in the preheated oven for 30 minutes.
4.   Drain the liquid from the faggots, either whisking the drained liquid onto the gravy powder, then heating and seasoning to taste, or, heating the brown sauce with a little of the drained liquid to produce a pouring sauce. Pour the resulting gravy over the faggots and return the casserole to the oven for 10 minutes. Sprinkle with chopped parsley and serve while piping hot.

PORK IN CIDER CASSEROLE

THE COCKLE WARREN
Hayling Island, Hampshire

Diane & David Skelton

.

A spicy mix of pork, tomatoes, cider and vegetables. Serve with cauliflower florets and jacket potatoes.

Serves 6

3 large onions, chopped
3 plump cloves garlic, crushed
45 ml (3 tbsp) olive oil
2 rashers bacon, diced
1 kg (2 lb) lean diced pork, cut into 2.5 cm (1 inch) dice
15 ml (1 tbsp) flour
either 1 × 397 g (14 oz) can of tomatoes
or 500 g (1 lb) tomatoes, skinned and
chopped and 5 ml (1 tsp) tomato purée
500 ml (1 pint) cider
seasoning
30 ml (2 tbsp) dried mixed herbs
1 bay leaf
bouquet garni
500 ml (1 pint) good chicken stock (see page 201)
5 ml (1 tsp) paprika
2 large carrots, peeled and chopped
1 green pepper, diced
250 ml (10 fl oz) double cream

To serve:
chopped parsley

1. In a large saucepan, fry the onion and garlic in the oil until transparent. Add the bacon and pork and continue to cook until the meat is sealed and browned.
2. Add the flour, followed by the tomatoes and cider. Bring the casserole to the boil, stirring constantly.
3. Stir in all the remaining ingredients, except the cream. Cover and simmer the casserole, stirring frequently, for 1¼–2 hours until the meat is tender. (Exact cooking time will depend on the cut of meat used – fillet will take far less time than loin, for example.)
4. Stir in the cream, taste and adjust seasoning before serving sprinkled with chopped parsley.

CHICKEN ON HORSEBACK

THE SCHOONER
Swansea, West Glamorgan

Raymond & Christine Parkman

·

Chicken breasts, filled with orange-soaked prunes, wrapped in bacon and set on a delicate cream and sherry sauce. Serve with green vegetables and jacket or new potatoes.

Serves 4

16 dried prunes
250 ml (10 fl oz) orange juice
4 chicken breasts, skinned and boned
4 rashers back bacon
100 g (4 oz) butter
250 ml (10 fl oz) medium sherry
5 ml (1 tsp) chopped fresh tarragon
50 g (2 oz) flour
250 ml (10 fl oz) milk
125 ml (5 fl oz) single cream
seasoning

1.   In a saucepan, soak the prunes in orange juice for half an hour, then simmer for 10 minutes. Drain and reserve the liquid.
2.   Preheat the oven to 180°C (350°F) mark 4.
3.   Between 2 sheets of greaseproof paper, flatten the chicken breasts by hitting with a meat mallet or rolling pin, until doubled in size. Peel off the paper, then place 4 prunes on top of each breast. Roll up the meat to enclose the prunes completely (they will look like fat cigars) and wrap a rasher of bacon around the outside to secure each parcel. If necessary, use cocktail sticks to fix the parcels.
4.   Melt half the butter in a frying pan and gently fry the chicken for 5 minutes on each side. Transfer the chicken parcels to an ovenproof dish, pour over the reserved orange juice and the sherry. Sprinkle with tarragon. Cover and bake in the hot oven for 20 minutes.
5.   Turn off the oven, remove the chicken parcels from the sauce and arrange on a serving plate. Cover with foil and return the chicken to the oven to keep warm while preparing the sauce.
6.   Melt the remaining butter, stir in the flour. Slowly add the chicken cooking juices and enough of the milk to make a smooth sauce. Add the cream and warm through. Taste and adjust seasoning.
7.   Pour the sauce around the chicken parcels and serve.

SEA COW CHICKEN SUPREME

SEA COW RESTAURANT
Weymouth, Dorset

Terry Woolcock

.

Breasts of chicken filled with crab meat, in a creamy mushroom sauce. Serve with lightly steamed sticks of mixed vegetables.

Serves 4

4 chicken breasts, skinned and boned

For the filling:
125 g (5 oz) crab meat, mixed white and brown
1 shallot, finely chopped
10 ml (2 tsp) chopped parsley
seasoning

For the sauce:
50 g (2 oz) clarified butter
50 g (2 oz) shallots, chopped
200 g (8 oz) mushrooms, sliced
100 g (4 oz) red pepper, diced
10 ml (2 tsp) flour
200 ml (8 fl oz) white wine
200 ml (8 fl oz) double cream
100 ml (4 fl oz) chopped, skinned tomatoes
60 ml (4 tbsp) fish stock (see page 200)
seasoning

1. In a bowl, mix together all the chicken filling ingredients.
2. Using a thin-bladed knife, cut a horizontal pocket in the side of each chicken breast, keeping the opening as small as possible and taking care not to cut through the meat. Fill the chicken with the crab mixture and seal the pockets closed with cocktail sticks.
3. Fry the chicken breasts for 15–20 minutes until almost cooked.
4. Add the shallots, mushrooms and pepper to the pan, stir and cook for 2 minutes until the pepper has softened. Stir in the flour, then gradually add the wine, cream, tomatoes, fish stock and seasoning. Bring to the boil and simmer for 3–5 minutes until the sauce has reduced and thickened. Taste and correct the seasoning.
5. Arrange the chicken breasts on a heatproof serving platter, remove the cocktail sticks and pour the sauce over the top. Place under a hot grill until the sauce starts to shine, then serve.

EAST COAST CHICKEN & SEAFOOD DELIGHT

UDNY ARMS HOTEL
Newburgh, Grampian

Denis & Jennifer Craig with chefs Jon Roberts and Karen Scott

Breasts of chicken filled with prawns and scallops, set on a bed of leeks and chives, with a wine and cream sauce. Serve with a selection of fresh green vegetables and lime-scented rice (see page 149).

Serves 6

For the chicken:
6 chicken breasts, boned and skinned
150 g (6 oz) peeled prawns
4 scallops, sliced
5 ml (1 tsp) lemon juice
seasoning

For the sauce:
25 g (1 oz) butter
15 g (½ oz) flour
250 ml (10 fl oz) white wine
seasoning
250 ml (10 fl oz) double cream
10 ml (2 tsp) snipped chives

For the leek bed:
2 medium leeks, sliced very thinly
30 ml (2 tbsp) snipped chives
25 g (1 oz) butter
45 ml (3 tbsp) white wine
seasoning

To serve:
snipped chives
peeled prawns

1.	Preheat the oven to 180°C (350°F) mark 4.
2.	Using a thin-bladed knife, cut a horizontal pocket in the side of each chicken breast, keeping the opening as small as possible and taking care not to cut through the flesh.

3. Mix the prawns and scallops together in a bowl with the lemon juice and a little seasoning. Fill the chicken breasts with this mixture, pulling the pocket closed and securing with a cocktail stick if necessary.

4. Arrange the chicken breasts on a baking sheet and cook in the preheated oven for 1 hour.

5. Prepare the sauce. Melt the butter in a saucepan, stir in the flour to form a roux and cook for 2 minutes until sandy in texture. Gradually stir in the white wine and seasoning. Bring to the boil and allow to reduce slightly. Stir in the double cream and chives, taste and correct seasoning, simmer until slightly thickened, then keep warm until required.

6. In a saucepan, prepare the leek bed by heating together the leeks, chives, butter and white wine for about 5 minutes until the leeks are just softened. Season.

7. Place a spoonful of leeks in the centre of each dinner plate and flatten slightly to form a nest for the chicken. Position the cooked chicken over the leeks (removing the cocktail sticks first), then flood the rim of the plate with hot cream sauce. Garnish with chives and prawns and serve immediately.

TARRAGON CHICKEN

CHAMBERLAIN'S BRASSERIE
Birmingham, West Midlands

Patrick Linehan

·

Chicken in a cream and white wine sauce, flavoured with tarragon. Serve with broccoli, glazed carrot batons and potato casserole (see page 148). If entertaining, cook the chicken and mix with the white sauce in advance, cover and refrigerate. Heat the casserole for 25–30 minutes in a hot oven before serving.

Serves 4–6

1 × 1.75 kg (3½ lb) chicken
15 g (½ oz) dried tarragon
2.5 ml (½ tsp) salt
12 peppercorns
4 bay leaves

For the sauce:
375 ml (15 fl oz) milk
1 bay leaf
sprig of thyme
1 small onion
2.5 ml (½ tsp) grated nutmeg
40 g (1½ oz) butter
40 g (1½ oz) flour
seasoning
125 ml (5 fl oz) double cream
50 ml (2 fl oz) white wine
1 egg yolk
15 g (½ oz) chopped tarragon

To serve:
sprigs of fresh tarragon

1.   In a large saucepan, cover the chicken with water, add the dried tarragon, salt, peppercorns and bay leaves. Bring to the boil and simmer for 45 minutes, turning the chicken twice during cooking to ensure all the meat is cooked.
2.   Drain the chicken on a wire rack, reserving 500 ml (1 pint) of cooking liquid for the sauce.
3.   While the chicken is boiling, prepare the sauce. Put the milk with the bay leaf, thyme, onion and nutmeg into a pan and bring to the boil. Remove from the heat, cover and leave to infuse for 15 minutes.
4.   In a separate pan, melt the butter, stir in the flour to form a roux and cook for 2 minutes until sandy in texture.
5.   Strain the milk and gradually add to the roux. Bring the sauce to the boil, stirring constantly, then allow to simmer for 2–3 minutes. Taste and adjust seasoning.
6.   Preheat the oven to 180°C (350°F) mark 4.
7.   Bring the reserved chicken stock to the boil, simmer until reduced to 125 ml (5 fl oz), then stir into the white sauce, along with the cream, white wine, egg yolk, and tarragon.
8.   Skin and remove the chicken meat from the bones. Place the meat in an ovenproof dish, keeping the chunks as large as possible. Pour the sauce over the chicken and heat in the warm oven for 10–12 minutes until the meat is hot and the sauce bubbling.
9.   Serve garnished with sprigs of fresh tarragon.

CHICKEN 'NARANJAS'

BRADFORD ARMS & RESTAURANT
Llanymynech, Shropshire
Michael & Ann Murphy

·

Breasts of chicken in a spiced orange and cinnamon sauce. Serve with salad and rice or noodles.

Serves 4

45 ml (3 tbsp) olive oil
4 breasts of chicken, skinned and boned
2 cloves garlic, crushed
1 onion, finely chopped
½ stick cinnamon
2 cloves
juice of 3 oranges
2 oranges, peeled and cut into segments
400 ml (16 fl oz) good chicken stock (see page 201)
pinch of saffron
15 ml (1 tbsp) raisins
15 g (½ oz) flaked almonds
5 ml (1 tsp) capers
seasoning

To serve:
chopped parsley

1.   Heat the oil in a deep-sided frying pan and cook the chicken breasts, turning frequently, for 10 minutes, until just golden.
2.   Add the garlic and onion to the pan and fry for 4–6 minutes until the onion has softened.
3.   Add the cinnamon, cloves, orange juice, orange segments, stock, saffron, raisins, almonds and capers to the pan. Season and allow to simmer for 15–20 minutes until the chicken is cooked and tender.
4.   Remove the chicken from the pan, arrange on a warmed serving dish, cover and keep warm.
5.   Increase the heat under the sauce and simmer until reduced, or stir in a little cornflour paste to thicken. Taste and adjust seasoning.
6.   Remove the cinnamon and cloves from the sauce. Spoon a little sauce over the chicken on its serving plate, arranging the orange segments, raisins and nuts attractively as garnish. Sprinkle the chicken with chopped parsley and serve, offering extra sauce in an accompanying jug.

CHICKEN SUPREME WITH MANGO, GINGER & CORIANDER

CRINGLETIE HOUSE HOTEL
Peebles, Borders

Stanley & Aileen Maguire

·

Chicken breasts in a creamy mango, ginger and coriander sauce. Serve with a selection of fresh vegetables and rice or new potatoes.

Serves 6

6 chicken breasts, skinned and boned
flour for dusting
seasoning
30 ml (2 tbsp) olive oil
25 g (1 oz) butter
50 ml (2 fl oz) chicken stock or white wine
1 mango, peeled and chopped
2.5 cm (1 inch) fresh ginger, grated
15 ml (1 tbsp) chopped fresh coriander
250 ml (10 fl oz) double cream

To serve:
sprigs of fresh coriander

1. Preheat the oven to 180°C (350°F) mark 4.
2. Dust the chicken with flour and seasoning.
3. Heat the oil and butter together in a frying pan until the butter has melted. Cook the chicken in the hot fat for 15–20 minutes until golden on all sides and just cooked through. Transfer the chicken to an ovenproof casserole dish.
4. Pour the stock or wine around the chicken and cook, covered, in the hot oven for 10 minutes while preparing the sauce.
5. Cook the mango in the fat left in the frying pan for 2 minutes, stir in the ginger and coriander and continue to cook for 1 minute. Stir in the cream, season to taste and cook until the sauce has slightly thickened.
6. Flood dinner plates with the sauce and place a chicken breast on top, garnish with sprigs of coriander and serve.

ITALIAN BAKED CHICKEN

SHEPHERD'S INN
Melmerby, Cumbria

Martin & Christine Baucutt

.

Chicken breasts baked in a red wine and tomato sauce, set in a nest of green tagliatelle. Serve with green beans, mange tout or a side salad.

Serves 6

6 chicken breasts, skinned and boned
seasoning
25 g (1 oz) butter
juice of 1 lemon
3 large onions, peeled and chopped
2–3 cloves garlic, crushed
4 sticks celery, chopped
1 large red pepper, sliced
5 ml (1 tsp) oregano
either 1 × 397 g (14 oz) can of tomatoes
or 500 g (1 lb) tomatoes, skinned and chopped and 5 ml (1 tsp) tomato purée
250 ml (10 fl oz) red wine
25 g (1 oz) cornflour
250 g (10 oz) fresh green tagliatelle

1.   Preheat the oven to 180°C (350°F) mark 4.
2.   Sprinkle the chicken portions with seasoning. Melt the butter in a large frying pan and fry the chicken until golden brown on all sides.
3.   Arrange the chicken in a casserole dish and pour over the lemon juice, cover and keep to one side while preparing the sauce.
4.   Place the onion, garlic, celery, red pepper and oregano in the frying pan used to cook the chicken, and cook for 5 minutes until the onion is transparent. Stir in the tomatoes and red wine. Bring to the boil, then pour this sauce over the chicken portions.
5.   Cover the casserole and bake in the preheated oven for 25–30 minutes until the chicken is tender.
6.   Mix the cornflour to a smooth paste with 25 ml (1 fl oz) water. Add the paste to the casserole and stir until the sauce has thickened. Taste and adjust seasoning.
7.   Cook the tagliatelle in plenty of boiling salted water until just tender. Drain, rinse and arrange on 6 warmed serving plates to form little nests. Top each with a portion of chicken and a spoonful of sauce.

CHICKEN DROFNATS

WYNDHAM ARMS
Clearwell, Gloucestershire
John Stanford with chef Paul Cooke

Chicken breasts stuffed with garlic and parsley butter, wrapped in bacon and parcelled in puff pastry. Serve with a creamy mushroom or spicy tomato sauce, fresh vegetables and mashed potatoes.

Serves 6

6 chicken breasts, boned and skinned
75 g (3 oz) butter
2 cloves garlic, crushed
15 g (½ oz) chopped parsley
seasoning
6 rashers unsmoked, rindless streaky bacon
500 g (1 lb) puff pastry
1 egg, lightly beaten

1. Preheat the oven to 220°C (425°F) mark 7.
2. Place the chicken breasts between 2 sheets of greaseproof paper and flatten slightly by hitting with a meat mallet or rolling pin.
3. Mix the butter, garlic and parsley together in a bowl and season. Place a good dollop of the butter mixture in the middle of each chicken breast, then roll up into a sausage shape, completely enclosing the butter. Wrap a rasher of bacon around each breast.
4. On a lightly floured surface, roll out the pastry until fairly thin and divide into 6 pieces. Wrap each chicken breast individually in pastry, moisten the edges with egg to seal and pinch the joining seam together to form a completely enclosed parcel. Decorate the top with pastry trimmings. Arrange the parcels on a baking sheet and brush with a little beaten egg.
5. Bake in the preheated oven for 25 minutes (the pastry should be risen and golden), then cover with foil or buttered paper and continue to cook for a further 20 minutes. Serve immediately with vegetables and sauce.

CHICKEN ALESCOMBE

OLD HALL HOTEL
Buxton, Derbyshire

Mrs Louise Potter with chef Mr J.R. Lath

Strips of chicken lightly fried in garlic butter with tarragon, mushrooms and prawns. Serve with fried onion rings (see page 153) and lime-scented rice (see page 149).

Serves 6

4 × 200 g (8 oz) chicken breasts, skinned and boned
65 g (2½ oz) butter
4 cloves garlic
10 ml (2 tsp) chopped tarragon
seasoning
150 g (6 oz) button mushrooms, sliced
75 g (3 oz) peeled prawns
15 ml (1 tbsp) chopped parsley

To serve:
lime-scented rice (see page 149)
chopped parsley
onion rings (see page 153)

1.   Slice the chicken, cutting about 10 slices from each breast.
2.   Melt the butter in a large frying pan and fry the chicken for 2 minutes. Add the garlic, tarragon and seasoning and cook for a further 2 minutes, stirring constantly. Add the mushrooms and prawns, and continue to cook until the mushrooms have softened.
3.   Arrange the cooked rice on a serving dish and top with the chicken. Sprinkle with parsley and dot with the prepared onion rings. Serve immediately.

CHICKEN ON GREEN LENTILS

THE COCKLE WARREN
Hayling Island, Hampshire
Diane & David Skelton
.

Baked chicken portions set on an unusual green lentil sauce. Serve
with a selection of crisp green vegetables.

Serves 4

50 g (2 oz) butter
30 ml (2 tbsp) olive oil
4 large chicken portions
1 onion, finely chopped
2 cloves garlic, crushed
½ green pepper, finely chopped
½ red pepper, finely chopped
2 rashers lean bacon, diced
175 ml (7 fl oz) white wine
750 ml (1½ pints) good chicken stock (see page 201)
90 g (3½ oz) green lentils, washed and soaked overnight
either 1 × 397 g (14 oz) can of tomatoes
or 500 g (1 lb) tomatoes, peeled and chopped and 5 ml (1 tsp) tomato
purée
15 ml (1 tbsp) dried mixed herbs
seasoning

To serve:
15 ml (1 tbsp) chopped parsley
½ bunch watercress, washed
1 lemon, cut into wedges

1. Preheat the oven to 180°C (350°F) mark 4.
2. Heat the butter and oil together in a large frying pan and fry the
chicken portions until just turning brown.
3. Remove the chicken from the pan and place, uncovered, on a
baking tray in the hot oven for 30 minutes until cooked through.
4. Meanwhile prepare the sauce. In the butter used to cook the
chicken, fry the onion, garlic, peppers and bacon together until the
onion is transparent. Add the white wine, bring to the boil and allow
to reduce slightly.
5. Add the stock, drained lentils, tomatoes and herbs, bring to the
boil and simmer for 20–30 minutes, until the lentils are tender. Add a
little more stock, if necessary, to give a pouring consistency.

6. Taste the sauce and season as necessary – only add salt when the lentils are cooked as adding salt beforehand will toughen the lentil husks.
7. Spoon the sauce onto individual serving plates, place a chicken portion in the centre of each plate and sprinkle with chopped parsley. Garnish with watercress and lemon wedges and serve immediately.

GLOUCESTER PIES

THE GEORGE INN
Cambridge, Gloucestershire

Alistair & Jane Deas with chef Josephine Nelmes

Individual pies filled with chicken, ham and hard-boiled egg, set in a parsley sauce and topped with a puff pastry crust. Serve with a mixed side salad and French bread.

Serves 4

75 g (3 oz) butter
25 g (1 oz) flour
500 ml (1 pint) milk
60 ml (4 tbsp) chopped parsley
seasoning
300 g (12 oz) cooked chicken meat, diced
200 g (8 oz) cooked ham, diced
4 hard-boiled eggs, peeled and chopped
500 g (1 lb) puff pastry
milk or beaten egg to glaze

1. Melt the butter in a saucepan, stir in the flour to form a roux and cook for 2 minutes until sandy in texture. Gradually add the milk, stirring constantly. Bring to the boil and allow to simmer for 2–3 minutes. Add parsley, season to taste and allow to cool.
2. Divide the chicken, ham and hard-boiled egg between 4 individual pie dishes. Cover the pie filling with parsley sauce.
3. On a lightly floured surface, roll out the pastry and use to cover the pies. Wet the edges of each pie dish to ensure a tight seal and decorate the tops with the pastry trimmings.
4. Refrigerate the pies while the oven heats to 220°C (425°F) mark 7.
5. Brush the pies with milk or beaten egg and bake in the hot oven for 15–20 minutes until the crust is golden brown.

FRESH CHICKEN CASSEROLE WITH LEMON & CHIVES

THE HARROW
West Ilsley, Berkshire

Mrs Heather Humphreys
.

A light, fresh-flavoured chicken casserole, perfect for spring and summer. Serve with a selection of vegetables and fresh pasta.

Serves 8

100 g (4 oz) butter
1 large onion, chopped
2 carrots, peeled and sliced
2 sticks celery, chopped
2 × 1.5 kg (3 lb) chickens, jointed, or 8 large chicken portions
250 ml (10 fl oz) white wine
750 ml (1½ pints) good chicken stock (see page 201)
juice and grated zest of 2 lemons
seasoning
60 ml (4 tbsp) snipped chives
10 ml (2 tsp) arrowroot
60 ml (4 tbsp) single cream

To serve:
1 lemon, peeled and cut into rings
chive flowers (optional)

1. Preheat the oven to 180°C (350°F) mark 4.
2. In a large saucepan, melt the butter and sauté the onion, carrots and celery until the onion is transparent. Add the chicken portions and continue to cook for about 10 minutes until browned.
3. Add the white wine, chicken stock, lemon zest and juice. Bring to the boil. Skim off any fat that rises to the surface and season.
4. Transfer to an ovenproof casserole dish, cover and bake for 1 hour in the hot oven, adding half the chives 10 minutes before the end.
5. Take the chicken out of the sauce and arrange on a warmed serving dish, cover and keep warm while finishing the sauce.
6. Mix the arrowroot to a paste with a little cold water, add to the sauce and heat through until thickened slightly, stirring constantly. Add the cream and adjust seasoning to taste.
7. Pour the sauce over the chicken portions and sprinkle with the remaining chives. Serve immediately, garnished with rings of lemon and chive flowers if available.

LOW HALL TURKEY ESCALOPES

LOW HALL COUNTRY GUESTHOUSE
Lorton, Cumbria

Dani Edwards

.

Turkey escalopes, baked with herbs, honey and lemon juice, topped with grapes. Serve with creamed spinach, carrot batons and pasta.

Serves 4

4 × 150 g (6 oz) turkey escalopes
seasoning
butter for frying
15 ml (1 tbsp) chopped mint
15 ml (1 tbsp) chopped thyme
30 ml (2 tbsp) lemon juice
30 ml (2 tbsp) honey
16 seedless black grapes, quartered
2 seedless white grapes, halved

1. Place each turkey escalope between 2 pieces of greaseproof paper and hit with a meat mallet or rolling pin to flatten slightly. Season each escalope.
2. Preheat the oven to 180°C (350°F) mark 4.
3. Heat the butter in a frying pan and use to seal the escalopes quickly. Transfer the turkey, together with the pan juices, to a shallow ovenproof dish. Sprinkle the herbs, lemon juice and honey over the turkey, cover and bake in the hot oven for 25 minutes.
4. Arrange the turkey escalopes on a warmed serving plate, top with the grapes, arranged to look like the petals of a flower, and a spoonful of the cooking liquid. Serve immediately.

GIN & LIME DUCK

LA VIEILLE AUBERGE
Battle, East Sussex

Trevor Keith & Jean Woolley

.

Grilled duck breasts with a sharp lime and gin sauce. Serve with a fresh vegetable selection and sauté or potato casserole (see page 148).

Serves 4

4 duck breasts or duck portions
125 ml (5 fl oz) good chicken or game stock
60 ml (4 tbsp) lime marmalade or preserve
juice and finely grated zest of 2 limes
45 ml (3 tbsp) gin
seasoning
25 g (1 oz) butter

To serve:
1 lime, cut into rings

1.   Place the duck breasts, fat side up, in a dry frying pan. Cook under a hot grill for 10 minutes, to extract the fat and brown the skin. Turn over and cook for 2 minutes flesh side up, then remove the frying pan from the grill and finish cooking on the hob to taste (well done, medium or rare). Remove the duck from the pan, cover and keep warm while preparing the sauce.
2.   Pour off all the fat from the pan. Add the stock and stir, scraping the duck juices from the base of the pan. The duck juices should make the sauce turn dark brown, if not add 5 ml (1 tsp) dark soy sauce to give colour.
3.   Add the marmalade and stir until melted, then add the lime juice, grated zest, gin and seasoning. Cut the butter into small pieces and whisk into the sauce, using a balloon whisk. Return the duck breasts to the pan, bring the sauce to the boil and simmer for 3 minutes until the sauce has thickened slightly. Taste and adjust seasoning.
4.   Arrange the duck on a serving platter, spoon a little sauce over each breast and garnish with twists of lime. Serve any extra sauce in a warmed jug.

UDNY DUCK

UDNY ARMS HOTEL
Newburgh, Grampian

Denis & Jennifer Craig with chefs Jon Roberts & Karen Scott

.

Breasts of duck, stuffed with a mixture of fresh mango and ginger, set on a spicy cashew nut sauce. Serve with green beans and seasoned boiled rice.

Serves 6

6 duck breasts

For the stuffing:
1 small onion, finely chopped
25 g (1 oz) fresh root ginger, finely chopped
½ ripe mango, peeled and chopped
seasoning

For the sauce:
25 g (1 oz) butter
2 shallots, chopped
1 clove garlic, crushed
100 g (4 oz) cashew nuts
1.25 cm (½ inch) fresh root ginger, grated
10 ml (2 tsp) coriander seed
5 ml (1 tsp) cumin seed
2 cloves
3 cardamom pods, husks removed
250 ml (10 fl oz) double cream
juice of 1 lime
seasoning

To serve:
1½ mangoes, peeled and thinly sliced
sprigs of fresh coriander

1.　Preheat the oven to 190°C (375°F) mark 5.
2.　Using a thin-bladed knife, cut a horizontal pocket in the side of each duck breast, keeping the opening as small as possible and taking care not to cut through the flesh. With a fork, pierce the fatty skin of the duck several times.
3.　In a bowl, mix the onion, ginger, mango and seasoning and use to fill the duck breasts, closing each pocket with a cocktail stick.
4.　Place the breasts, fat side uppermost, in a roasting tin and cook in the hot oven for 1 hour, until the fat is crisp and the juices run clear. Drain the fat from the pan several times during roasting.
5.　Meanwhile, prepare the sauce. Melt the butter in a frying pan and fry the shallots and garlic for 5 minutes. Add nuts and ginger.
6.　In a spice mill or coffee grinder, grind the coriander seed, cumin, cloves and cardamom seeds to a fine powder and add to the frying pan. Fry for several minutes until the spices give off a warm pungent aroma. Stir in the cream and lime juice, taste and correct seasoning.
7.　Remove the cocktail sticks from the duck breasts and slice each into 4 to expose the stuffing. Flood warmed dinner plates with the sauce and arrange the sliced duck in a fan to one side of the plate. Serve while piping hot, garnished with fresh mango slices and coriander leaves.

PARTRIDGES IN CIDER SAUCE

NETHERWOOD HOTEL
Grange-over-Sands, Cumbria

Messrs J.D. & M.P. Fallowfield with chef Mr M. Fowler

·

Partridges braised in a herb and cider sauce. Serve with braised red cabbage or creamed spinach and game chips.

Serves 4

4 partridges, cleaned and halved
salt
50 g (2 oz) lard or dripping
100 g (4 oz) bacon, diced
500 g (1 lb) button onions, peeled
2 carrots, peeled and sliced
15 ml (1 tbsp) flour
300 ml (12 fl oz) dry cider
1 sprig each of thyme, parsley and marjoram, tied together
1 bay leaf
pinch of grated nutmeg
seasoning

To serve:
chopped parsley

1.   Rub the skin of the partridges with salt.
2.   Heat the fat in a large saucepan, add the partridges and fry until lightly browned all over. Remove the birds from the pan and keep to one side.
3.   Add the bacon, onions and carrots to the pan, stir in the flour and cook for 2 minutes, stirring constantly. Pour in the cider and add the herbs, bay leaf, nutmeg and seasoning, mixing thoroughly.
4.   Return the partridges to the pan, cover and cook over a gentle heat for 1–1½ hours until the partridges are tender.
5.   Remove the bunch of herbs and bay leaf from the pan, arrange the partridges, with a little sauce, on individual plates or 1 large serving dish, sprinkle with chopped parsley and serve.

Rosettes of Lamb Daniel Patrick (page 70)

BRAISED VENISON CUTLETS WITH JUNIPER & BLACK CHERRY SAUCE

THE PHEASANT INN
Bassenthwaite Lake, Cumbria

Mr W.E. Barrington Wilson

·

Venison braised in a creamy sauce, flavoured with black cherries and juniper berries. Serve with redcurrant jelly and a selection of lightly steamed fresh vegetables. This recipe can also be used to prepare lamb cutlets.

Serves 4

50 g (2 oz) butter
4 venison cutlets
100 g (4 oz) shallots, chopped
50 g (2 oz) juniper berries
250 ml (10 fl oz) red wine
seasoning
250 ml (10 fl oz) double cream
100 g (4 oz) stoned black cherries, fresh or canned

1. Preheat the oven to 180°C (350°F) mark 4.
2. Melt the butter in a flameproof casserole dish and gently fry the cutlets for about 10 minutes until browned on both sides.
3. Add the shallots, reduce the heat slightly and cook until they become soft and transparent. Add the juniper berries, red wine and seasoning to the pan, stir, cover and cook in the preheated oven for 30 minutes.
4. Remove the casserole from the oven and stir in the cream and cherries. On the hob, bring the casserole to the boil and simmer for 10–12 minutes until the sauce has reduced and thickened slightly.
5. Taste and adjust seasoning and serve while piping hot.

Note: You may prefer to remove some of the juniper berries with a slotted spoon before serving this dish, leaving only a few in the sauce for decoration.

Duck & Cherry Pie (page 99)

ANN LONG'S DUCK BREASTS

LONG'S RESTAURANT
Truro, Cornwall

Ian & Ann Long

.

Oven-baked duck breasts, wrapped in bacon and served on a red wine sauce with blackcurrant purée. Serve with spiced white cabbage (see page 152), broad beans with mustard sauce (see page 152) and parsley potatoes.

Serves 4

For the blackcurrant purée:
175 g (7 oz) blackcurrants, fresh or frozen
5 ml (1 tsp) water
5 ml (1 tsp) caster sugar
40 ml (1½ fl oz) red wine vinegar
40 ml (1½ fl oz) redcurrant jelly
15 ml (1 tbsp) crème de cassis
100 ml (4 fl oz) chicken stock
25 g (1 oz) butter

For the red wine sauce:
150 ml (6 fl oz) red wine
150 ml (6 fl oz) duck or chicken stock (see page 201)
65 ml (2½ fl oz) brown sauce (see page 203)
2.5 ml (½ tsp) redcurrant jelly
1.25 ml (¼ tsp) Worcestershire Sauce
seasoning
either 2 × 2.5 kg (5 lb) fresh ducks and remove the breasts yourself
(saving the carcasses to prepare duck stock)
or 4 pre-cut duck breasts
4 slices middle back rindless bacon
oil

1. First prepare the blackcurrant purée which will keep for up to 5 days in the refrigerator.
2. Put half the blackcurrants together with the water and sugar into a saucepan. Cook until the fruit is tender.
3. In a small saucepan, reduce the vinegar and redcurrant jelly to a syrup, pour over the cooked blackcurrants, add the crème de cassis and chicken stock.
4. Remove the pan from the heat. Liquidise and sieve the blackcurrant sauce, add the remaining raw blackcurrants and refrigerate.

5.   Prepare the red wine sauce. Heat the red wine in a small pan until reduced to half volume. Add the stock, brown sauce, redcurrant jelly and Worcestershire Sauce, whisking with a balloon whisk until smooth. Season and cover until ready to serve.

6.   Now cook the duck. Run the blunt side of a knife over each rasher of bacon to stretch it gently. Using fingers and a small knife, carefully pull and roll away the skin from each duck breast, cutting the tissues to release it. Trim off the fat and remove the tubes and white thread in each fillet. Cut each breast in half widthways and fold over.

7.   Wrap a rasher of bacon around each breast and secure with string. Brush with a little oil.

8.   Heat the oven to 200°C (400°F) mark 6.

9.   Heat a little oil in a frying pan and fry the duck parcels until the bacon is brown on all sides. Remove the parcels from the oil and arrange on a baking tray. Cook at the top of the hot oven for 20–25 minutes until the duck meat feels firm but the juices still run pink. Untie the string and leave the meat to rest while you reheat the sauces.

10.   Whisk the butter, cut into small cubes, into the blackcurrant sauce as it heats. This will give the sauce a lovely shine.

11.   Cut each piece of duck across the grain into 3 slices. Flood the plates with red wine sauce, arrange the duck on top and spoon the blackcurrant purée to one side of the meat. Serve immediately.

DUCK & CHERRY PIE

MAWDESLEYS EATING HOUSE
Mawdesley, Lancashire
Edward Newton – Manager

.

Rich, individual, duck and black cherry pies. Alternatively, prepare the same filling and use to make one large pie in a 1 litre (2 pint) pie dish, in which case you will need only 250 g (10 oz) puff pastry. Serve with leeks tossed in garlic butter and parsley potatoes.

Serves 4

2 kg (4 lb) boiling duck
2 bay leaves
25 g (1 oz) butter
1 onion, chopped
1 clove garlic, chopped
1 stick celery, chopped
1 carrot, chopped
25 g (1 oz) flour
15 ml (1 tbsp) tomato purée
1 bouquet garni
250 ml (10 fl oz) red wine
either 1 × 375 g (15 oz) can stoned black cherries
or 500 g (1 lb) black cherries, stoned, and 100 ml (4 fl oz) water
125 ml (5 fl oz) port
75 g (3 oz) redcurrant jelly
seasoning
500 g (1 lb) puff pastry
milk or beaten egg to glaze

1.   Cover the duck and bay leaves with water in a large pan, bring to the boil and allow to simmer for 2 hours until the duck is cooked. Drain the duck and leave to cool, saving 500 ml (1 pint) of the cooking liquid. Allow to cool, then skim off the fat.
2.   Prepare the sauce. Melt the butter in a saucepan and use to sauté the onion, garlic, celery and carrot until the onion is transparent. Stir in the flour and tomato purée, then gradually add the reserved duck cooking liquid. Add the bouquet garni, bring the mixture to the boil and allow to simmer, uncovered, for 15 minutes, stirring occasionally. Sieve, saving only the liquid.
3.   Meanwhile, in another pan, heat together the red wine, juice of the cherries (or the water) and the port. Simmer until reduced to half the volume. Stir in the redcurrant jelly and sieved sauce. Taste and season, then simmer for 5 minutes.
4.   Skin and strip the meat from the duck – the larger the pieces of duck meat the better.
5.   Stir the duck and cherries into the prepared sauce and spoon into a 1 litre (2 pint) pie dish or divide between 4 individual pie dishes. Leave to cool before covering with pastry.
6.   On a lightly floured surface, roll out the pastry and use to cover the pie(s), moistening the rim of the dish to seal securely. Decorate with pastry trimmings, then refrigerate until required.
7.   Preheat the oven to 230°C (450°F) mark 8. Brush the pastry with milk or egg to glaze and bake in the preheated oven for 20–30 minutes until the pastry is golden brown.

SOMERSET SOUSED DUCK

DEEPLEIGH FARM HOTEL
Langley Marsh, Somerset

Linda & Lester Featherstone

Duck portions in gin and cider sauce. Serve with sautéed mushrooms and croquette potatoes.

Serves 4

1 × 2 kg (4 lb) duck, jointed
30 ml (2 tbsp) butter
30 ml (2 tbsp) olive oil
2 onions, finely chopped
2 medium carrots, peeled and sliced
2 sticks celery, sliced
2 cloves garlic, crushed
100 g (4 oz) unsmoked bacon
60 ml (4 tbsp) gin
600 ml (1¼ pints) dry cider
10 juniper berries, crushed
bouquet garni
grated zest of 1 lemon
seasoning
10 ml (2 tsp) arrowroot

To serve:
chopped parsley

1. Preheat the oven to 180°C (350°F) mark 4.
2. Prick the skin of the duck portions with a fork and place skin side up on a roasting tin. Cook in the preheated oven for 35 minutes.
3. In a flameproof casserole dish, heat the butter and olive oil together and use to sauté the onions, carrots, celery, garlic and bacon until the onion is transparent. Add the gin, cider, juniper berries, bouquet garni and lemon zest. Season to taste.
4. Remove the duck from the oven and place the portions in the sauce leaving as much fat as possible in the roasting tray.
5. Reduce the oven temperature to 150°C (300°F) mark 2 and cook the casserole, covered, for 1 hour until the duck is tender.
6. Remove the bouquet garni. Mix the arrowroot to a paste with a little cold water and stir into the sauce. Heat, stirring constantly until the sauce thickens slightly, then sprinkle with chopped parsley and serve immediately.

THE WILD BUNCH

LEADBURN INN
West Linton, Lothian

Mr & Mrs Thomson with chef Mr George Wilson
.

A casserole of venison, rabbit and pheasant in a slightly sweet cranberry and whisky sauce, accompanied by game chips. Serve with peas, buttered carrot batons and jacket potatoes.

Serves 10–12

1 rabbit, cut into portions
1 pheasant, cut into portions
1 kg (2 lb) venison, diced
1 large onion, chopped
4 large carrots, chopped
200 g (8 oz) mushrooms
15 ml (1 tbsp) tomato purée
1 chicken stock cube
seasoning
500 g (1 lb) cranberry sauce
125 ml (5 fl oz) whisky
10 ml (2 tsp) cornflour

To serve:
chopped fresh rosemary
game chips

1.   In a large saucepan, cover the rabbit and pheasant with water. Cover the pan, bring to the boil and allow to simmer for 1½–2 hours until the meat is cooked.
2.   Drain the stock from the rabbit and pheasant into a clean saucepan and allow the meat to cool.
3.   Add the venison to the rabbit cooking liquid, cover and simmer for 45 minutes, then add the onion, carrots, mushrooms, tomato purée and chicken stock cube. Season and continue to simmer for ½–1 hour until the venison is tender.
4.   Strip the meat from the rabbit and pheasant bones.
5.   Add the cranberry sauce, whisky, rabbit and pheasant meat to the venison pan. Simmer for 15 minutes, taste and correct seasoning.
6.   Mix the cornflour to a paste with water and stir, a little at a time, into the stew, to thicken to your taste (you may not require any thickening at all).
7.   Ladle into deep plates or bowls and serve garnished with rosemary and game chips.

GREIG'S HALIBUT

GREIG'S RESTAURANT
Barnes, London
Malcolm Greig with chef Malcolm Douglas

•

Steamed halibut steaks, topped with smoked salmon and lime hollandaise, garnished with sprigs of fresh dill and black lumpfish roe. Serve with a mixed salad and parsley potatoes.

Serves 4

seasoning
4 × 150 g (6 oz) halibut steaks
4 slices smoked salmon
4 slices lime

For the hollandaise:
4 egg yolks
200 g (8 oz) butter
grated zest of ½ lime
seasoning

To serve:
4 sprigs of fresh dill
20 ml (4 tsp) black lumpfish roe

1. Prepare the hollandaise. In a double boiler or bowl set over a pan of hot water, beat the egg yolks with a balloon whisk until stiff and slightly pale. Slowly whisk in the butter, cut into cubes, followed by the lime zest and seasoning. Cover and keep warm until required.
2. Season the halibut. Steam the steaks over boiling water or court bouillon (using a steamer, or wire rack sitting on a roasting tin) for 8–10 minutes until the fish is cooked. Actual cooking time will depend on the thickness of the steaks used. Arrange the fish on a large heatproof plate.
3. Place a slice of smoked salmon on top of the halibut and cover with hollandaise sauce. Set a slice of lime on each portion and cook under a hot grill, until the sauce shines and turns golden.
4. Spoon a little lumpfish roe onto each piece of fish and garnish with a sprig of dill before serving.

ESPALIER OF SALMON

NORMANTON PARK HOTEL
Rutland Water, Leicestershire

Mr & Mrs A.F. Chamberlain

.

Poached fillets of salmon topped with individual pastry lattices, in a cream and Pernod sauce. Serve with steamed carrot or courgette sticks and creamed potatoes.

Serves 6

200 g (8 oz) spinach
250 g (10 oz) puff pastry
1 egg, lightly beaten
6 × 150 g (6 oz) salmon fillets
125 ml (5 fl oz) Pernod
250 ml (10 fl oz) fish stock (see page 200)
50 g (2 oz) mushrooms
500 ml (20 fl oz) cream

1. Preheat the oven to 220°C (425°F) mark 7.
2. Blanch the spinach for 1 minute in boiling water, drain and refresh in cold water.
3. On a lightly floured surface, roll out the puff pastry until thin. Cut into strips 0.5 cm (¼ inch) wide. Use the strips to create 6 lattice tops, approximately the same size as the salmon fillets, by laying several horizontal strips out on a baking sheet and threading the vertical strips above and below them. Brush liberally with egg to seal the lattice and bake in the preheated oven for 15 minutes or until cooked and golden. Carefully lift from the baking sheet and keep warm.
4. Heat the salmon, Pernod and fish stock together in a deep frying pan or saucepan, simmer for 1 minute, cover and turn off the heat. Leave to cool for 5 minutes in the liquor, by which time the salmon should be cooked to perfection.
5. Spread the spinach over the base of a warm serving plate.
6. Remove the salmon from the cooking liquor and arrange on the serving plate over the spinach. Sprinkle a spoonful of cooking liquid over each piece of salmon, to prevent it drying out, cover and keep warm.
7. Bring the salmon cooking liquid to the boil and simmer until reduced by half. Add the mushrooms and cream, stir and season.
8. As soon as the sauce is at an acceptable consistency, pour it into a warm jug or sauce boat. Uncover the salmon, place a warm pastry lattice on top of each fillet and serve.

BRIGHTON SALMON

CHARDONNAY RESTAURANT
Brighton, Sussex

Karl & Rita Simpson

.

Fillets of salmon in a butter and sweet Sauternes sauce. Serve with tossed green or wild rice salad (see page 154) and sautéed potatoes.

Serves 4

4 × 150–200 g (6–8 oz) salmon cutlets or escalopes
500 ml (20 fl oz) court bouillon (see page 202)
100 g (4 oz) butter
50 g (2 oz) Spanish onions, thinly sliced
125 ml (5 fl oz) Sauternes or other sweet wine
50 ml (2 fl oz) beef stock (see page 200)
5 ml (1 tsp) chopped tarragon
seasoning

1. Place the salmon and court bouillon in a large saucepan, bring to the boil, simmer for 1 minute, cover and turn off the heat. By the time your sauce is prepared the salmon should be cooked to perfection.
2. In a frying pan, melt half the butter and fry the onions for 5–8 minutes until soft. Add the wine, stock, tarragon and seasoning. Bring to the boil, then, using a balloon whisk, whisk in the remaining butter, cut into small pieces. As the butter melts into the sauce it should thicken slightly. Taste and adjust seasoning.
3. Arrange the salmon on a warm serving plate, pour over the sauce and serve immediately.

SALMON CASTLE TUDOR

OLD HALL HOTEL
Buxton. Derbyshire

Mrs Louise Potter with chef Mr J.R. Lath

.

Salmon steaks, baked with asparagus, pears and cucumber, topped by a pastry crust and set on a raspberry cream sauce. Serve with braised fennel or lightly steamed green vegetables and new potatoes.

Serves 4

150 ml (6 fl oz) white wine
8 bay leaves
5 ml (1 tsp) chopped parsley
5 ml (1 tsp) chopped sage
5 ml (1 tsp) chopped rosemary
5 ml (1 tsp) chopped basil
4 × 200 g (8 oz) salmon steaks, skinned
8 spears fresh asparagus, peeled
2 dessert pears, peeled, cored and sliced
16 slices cucumber
seasoning
250 g (10 oz) puff pastry
1 egg, lightly beaten

For the sauce:
150 ml (6 fl oz) double cream
300 g (12 oz) raspberries

To serve:
sprigs of fresh fennel

1. Preheat the oven to 220°C (425°F) mark 7.
2. Place the wine, bay leaves, herbs and salmon steaks together in a large saucepan with enough water to cover the fish. Bring to the boil and simmer for 3 minutes. With a slotted spoon, remove the salmon from the stock and arrange on a baking sheet.
3. Plunge the asparagus into the hot stock and simmer for 2 minutes until softened. Drain.
4. Arrange the asparagus, pear and cucumber slices over the salmon steaks and season.
5. On a lightly floured surface, roll out the pastry until fairly thin and cut into pieces roughly the same shape as the salmon, but 2.5 cm (1 inch) bigger all round.
6. Pour 10 ml (2 tsp) stock over each salmon steak before topping with a piece of pastry. Pinch the pastry into the base of the baking sheet to form a seal, decorate with pastry off-cuts and brush with egg.
7. Bake in the preheated oven for 25–30 minutes, until the pastry is golden brown.
8. To prepare the sauce, lightly whip the cream until starting to thicken, then beat in the raspberries. The sauce will thin as the raspberries release their juice.
9. As soon as it is cooked, place the salmon in the centre of a warmed serving plate and surround with the raspberry cream. Garnish with the fennel sprigs and serve immediately.

COULIBIAC OF SALMON

PARKMOUNT HOUSE HOTEL
Forres, Grampian

Angie & David Steer

.

A traditional Russian salmon pie. Serve hot with bowls of soured cream and steamed green beans, or cold with a selection of salads.

Serves 8–10

1 kg (2 lb) fresh salmon
500 ml (1 pint) court bouillon (see page 202)
50 g (2 oz) butter
1 large onion, finely chopped
225 g (9 oz) mushrooms, sliced
2 hard-boiled eggs, peeled and chopped
30 ml (2 tbsp) chopped parsley
seasoning
750 g (1½ lb) puff pastry
butter for greasing
50 g (2 oz) rice, cooked in chicken stock
1 egg, lightly beaten

1. Place the salmon and court bouillon together in a saucepan. Bring to the boil and simmer for 3–5 minutes until the salmon is cooked. Turn off the heat and leave to cool.
2. In a saucepan, melt the butter and sauté the onion until soft, add the mushrooms and cook for a further minute.
3. In a bowl, mix together the eggs, parsley and seasoning.
4. Skin, remove the bones and flake the cooled salmon.
5. Divide the pastry in half. On a lightly floured surface, roll out both pieces of pastry to form similar rectangles.
6. Place one pastry rectangle on a greased baking sheet, top with the rice, salmon, egg mixture and finally the onion mix, spreading each layer as evenly as possible to within a few centimetres of the pastry edge. Brush the edge of the pastry with the beaten egg and place the second pastry rectangle on top, pressing the edges together to seal.
7. Carefully run a knife over the top pastry layer to form an attractive pattern, without actually cutting through the pastry; these marks will be highlighted as the pastry cooks. Refrigerate until required.
8. Heat the oven to 200°C (400°F) mark 6.
9. Brush the pie with beaten egg, then bake in the hot oven for 40 minutes until the pastry is risen and golden. Carefully lift the coulibiac onto a serving plate and serve.

SALMON WITH GRAND MARNIER

SEA COW RESTAURANT
Weymouth, Dorset

Terry Woolcock

.

Fillets of salmon, baked in a cream and Grand Marnier sauce, with peppers and almonds. Serve with steamed strips of carrot, celery, courgette and fennel tossed in sesame seeds and boiled new potatoes, served in their skins.

Serves 4

25 g (1 oz) butter
1 clove garlic, crushed
7.5 g (¼ oz) chopped parsley
4 × 150 g (6 oz) salmon fillets, boned and skinned
125 ml (5 fl oz) white wine
25 g (1 oz) shallots, chopped
25 g (1 oz) spring onions, chopped
25 g (1 oz) yellow pepper, chopped
25 g (1 oz) orange pepper, chopped
15 ml (1 tbsp) flour
50 ml (2 fl oz) lemon juice
150 ml (6 fl oz) Grand Marnier
60 ml (4 tbsp) fish stock
150 ml (6 fl oz) double cream
50 g (2 oz) flaked almonds

To serve:
pepper rings

1. Melt the butter with garlic and parsley in a large frying pan, cook the salmon briefly on both sides to seal the fish, remove from the pan and keep to one side.
2. Pour the white wine into the pan, bring to the boil and simmer until reduced to only a third of the volume. Add the shallots, spring onions and peppers, stir and cook for 1 minute.
3. Stir in the flour and gradually add the lemon juice, Grand Marnier, fish stock and cream. Heat until bubbling. Replace the fish in the pan and add the almonds. Cook for 1½–2 minutes until the salmon is cooked through (depending on the thickness of the fish).
4. Carefully lift the fish onto warmed serving plates. Spoon a little sauce over the top, garnish with the peppers and serve, offering extra sauce in an accompanying jug.

YORKSHIRE DALES RAINBOW TROUT

BRIDGE HOTEL
Ripon, North Yorkshire
Allan Reinhard with chef Kevin Warner

.

Rainbow trout, flavoured with mushrooms, almonds and prawns. Serve with braised fennel, baked tomatoes and mashed or casseroled potatoes (see page 148).

Serves 4

100 g (4 oz) butter
30 ml (2 tbsp) olive oil
4 × 225–250 g (9–10 oz) rainbow trout, cleaned
100 g (4 oz) mushrooms, sliced
100 g (4 oz) blanched almonds
100 g (4 oz) prawns

To serve:
2 pimento-stuffed olives, halved
1 lemon, cut into wedges

1. In a large frying pan, heat together the butter and oil until the butter has melted. Add the trout and cook for 3–5 minutes on each side until the flesh is firm, cooked through and the skin is turning brown.
2. Add the mushrooms, almonds and prawns, and stir until the mushrooms have softened. Turn off the heat.
3. Carefully take the trout from the pan and arrange on a warmed serving dish. Remove the visible eye of each trout and replace with half a pimento-stuffed olive.
4. Spoon the mushrooms, prawns and almonds over the fish with a little butter and oil. Garnish with lemon wedges and serve immediately.

TROUT WITH LEEKS

OLD SWAN INN
Llantwit Major, South Glamorgan

Geoff & Myra Radford

.

Fillets of trout, poached in cream and flavoured with leeks. Serve with green beans and mashed or croquette potatoes.

Serves 4

4 small leeks
50 g (2 oz) butter
4 fresh trout, gutted and filleted
seasoning
500 ml (1 pint) double cream

1. Slice the white part of the leeks into thin rounds, leave the green leafy ends whole and wash both parts thoroughly.
2. Over a moderate heat, melt the butter in a large, lidded frying pan, without letting it burn. Arrange the fish fillets in the pan, skin side down, and sprinkle the leek rings over them. Season and pour the cream around the fish. As soon as the cream comes to the boil, reduce the heat and cover the pan. Leave to cook for 4 minutes.
3. Using a fish slice, carefully put the fish fillets together, so they form the shape of a whole fish once more, and arrange the green leek leaves over the top. Cover the pan and continue to cook for 2 minutes.
4. Carefully remove the fish from the pan and arrange on a warmed serving dish, cover and keep warm. Bring the sauce to the boil and stir until slightly thickened. Pour around the fish and serve immediately.

TURBOT WITH INK CAPS

BLANCHARDS SEAFOOD RESTAURANT
Bournemouth, Dorset

Jo Mitchell

.

Poached fillets of turbot set on a rich sauce of ink cap mushrooms. Fresh ink caps are available from late summer to autumn, the young button ones having the best flavour. Serve with a selection of green vegetables and creamed potatoes.

Serves 4

1.5 kg (3 lb) turbot, skinned and filleted
125 ml (5 fl oz) fish stock (see page 200)
125 ml (5 fl oz) white wine
200 g (8 oz) ink cap mushrooms
100 g (4 oz) unsalted butter
125 ml (5 fl oz) double cream
seasoning

To serve:
coriander leaves

1. Place the turbot, with half the stock and half the wine, in a saucepan. Cover and poach lightly for 10–12 minutes.
2. Wash the mushrooms and gently fry in half the butter in a separate saucepan. When just soft, remove 2 mushrooms for garnish. Increase the heat and pour the remaining stock and wine into the pan, bring to the boil and simmer until reduced to half volume.
3. Remove the turbot from its cooking liquid, cover and keep warm. Pour the fish cooking liquid into the mushroom pan, add the cream and simmer for 5 minutes. Liquidise and strain the sauce, stir in the remaining butter, cut into small pieces, and heat until the butter has melted. Taste and season the sauce.
4. Flood the base of 4 dinner plates with the sauce, place a piece of turbot in the centre of each plate and garnish with the reserved mushrooms and coriander leaves. Serve immediately.

HALIBUT STEAKS WITH RHUBARB & MINT SAUCE

HENLEY HOTEL
Bigbury-on-Sea, Devon

Mrs L. Beer

·

Braised halibut steaks served with a sharp rhubarb and mint sauce. Serve with green beans or broccoli and sautéed potatoes. Serve this minted rhubarb sauce with other grilled fish steaks, such as cod.

Serves 4

4 × 150–200 g (6–8 oz) halibut steaks
25 g (1 oz) butter
125 ml (5 fl oz) fish stock (see page 201)
250 ml (10 fl oz) white wine
1 bay leaf
2 sticks celery, chopped
½ onion, chopped
500 g (1 lb) rhubarb, chopped
30 ml (2 tbsp) caster sugar
5 ml (1 tsp) chopped mint or coriander
seasoning

To serve:
sprigs of fennel or parsley
1 lemon, sliced

1. Place the halibut in a saucepan with the butter, stock, wine, bay leaf, celery and onion. Cover and bring to the boil, then gently simmer for 10–15 minutes (depending on the thickness of the steak) until the fish is just tender.
2. Carefully remove the fish from the pan and arrange on a warm serving dish, cover with foil and keep warm.
3. Strain the cooking liquid into another saucepan. Add the chopped rhubarb and sugar, bring to the boil and stir until the rhubarb has completely broken down. Add the mint or coriander, taste and correct the sugar and seasoning levels, then simmer for 2 minutes.
4. Garnish the halibut steaks with sprigs of fresh fennel or parsley and twists of lemon. Place a spoonful of the rhubarb sauce beside the fish and serve, offering extra sauce in an accompanying sauce boat.

Cornish Crab in Filo Pastry Bags (page 123)

SEA BASS WITH LIME

BLANCHARDS SEAFOOD RESTAURANT
Bournemouth, Dorset

Jo Mitchell
.

Sea bass baked with fennel, carrot, vermouth and fish stock. Serve with button mushrooms, courgettes and lime-scented rice (see page 149). To ease preparation, ask the fishmonger to bone and clean the sea bass through the back, for you.

Serves 4

4 × 500 g (1 lb) sea bass
1 bulb fennel
1 carrot, peeled
50 g (2 oz) butter
grated zest and juice of 2 limes
100 ml (4 fl oz) vermouth
100 ml (4 fl oz) fish stock (see page 201)
seasoning
10 ml (2 tsp) pink peppercorns

To serve:
1 lime, cut into wedges

1.   Preheat the oven to 220°C (425°F) mark 7.
2.   Scale and de-fin the bass. Bone and clean through the back.
3.   Cut the green feathery leaves from the fennel and save for the sauce. Cut the remaining fennel bulb and carrot into thin strips and fry in half the butter until just softened.
4.   Divide the carrot and fennel mixture into 4, placing a portion in the cavity of each fish.
5.   Arrange the bass in a roasting tin. Sprinkle lime zest and juice over the fish. Pour vermouth and fish stock into the pan, season and dot with the remaining butter. Cover with foil and bake in the preheated oven for 12–15 minutes.
6.   Remove the fish from the tin, arrange on a serving plate, cover and keep warm while preparing the sauce. Pour the fish cooking liquid into a saucepan and boil over a fierce heat for 10 minutes or until reduced to a third of the volume. Toss in the chopped fennel leaves and pink peppercorns.
7.   Pour the hot sauce over the fish, garnish with lime and serve.

RED SNAPPER IN CORIANDER

NETHERWOOD HOTEL
Grange-over-Sands, Cumbria

Messrs J.D. & M.P. Fallowfield with chef Mr M. Fowler

Red snapper with a crisp lime, coriander and breadcrumb crust. Serve with braised celery or fennel and leek and potato fritters (see page 148). Any fillet of white fish could be prepared using this recipe. Simply adjust the cooking time according to the thickness and density of the fish used.

Serves 4–6

1 kg (2 lb) red snapper, filleted
60 ml (4 tbsp) olive oil
60 ml (4 tbsp) lime or lemon juice
10 ml (2 tsp) salt
25 g (1 oz) breadcrumbs
1 clove garlic, crushed
90 ml (6 tbsp) chopped coriander leaves
5 ml (1 tsp) grated lime or lemon zest

1.   Rinse the fish fillets and pat dry on kitchen paper.
2.   Lightly brush a frying pan with a little of the oil and heat. Rub the fish with half the lime juice and 5 ml (1 tsp) of the salt. Place the fish in the pan, skin side down, add water just to cover the fish and simmer for 5 minutes, carefully turning twice during cooking.
3.   In another pan, heat together half the remaining oil, with the breadcrumbs, garlic, remaining salt, and all but 30 ml (2 tbsp) of the coriander. Cook, stirring constantly, until the crumbs are crisp and toasted.
4.   Mix the remaining lime juice and oil together.
5.   Remove the fish from the frying pan and place on the grill tray or on a heatproof serving dish. Spread the toasted crumb mix evenly over the fish flesh and grill for 7–10 minutes until the fish flakes easily when tested with a fork. Sprinkle the mixed oil and lime juice over the fish as it grills to prevent it drying out.
6.   Combine the remaining coriander and grated lime zest in a bowl.
7.   Carefully lift the fish onto warmed serving plates, sprinkle with coriander and lime mix and serve.

FILLETS OF PLAICE 'HANOVER STYLE'

BRADFORD ARMS & RESTAURANT
Llanymynech, Shropshire

Michael & Anne Murphy

.

Fillets of plaice, sautéed in butter, with a sauce of onion, smoked ham, parsley and white wine. Serve with a selection of fresh vegetables and buttered noodles.

Serves 4

150 g (6 oz) butter
1 medium onion, finely chopped
50 g (2 oz) thinly sliced smoked ham
15 ml (1 tbsp) chopped parsley
4 × 150–200 g (6–8 oz) plaice fillets
seasoning
100 ml (4 fl oz) white wine

To serve:
1 lemon, sliced

1.   Melt the butter in a large frying pan and fry the onion, ham and two thirds of the parsley for 10 minutes until the onion is transparent. Remove from the pan with a slotted spoon and reserve.
2.   Turn on the grill.
3.   Place the fish, skin side down, in the frying pan and fry for 2 minutes, basting with butter as it cooks.
4.   Place the frying pan under the hot grill and grill for 3 minutes until the fish is almost cooked through. Continue to baste during cooking.
5.   Raise the heat and allow the butter to burn slightly on the surface of the fish.
6.   Return the frying pan to the hob, season, pour in the wine and replace the ham, onion and parsley mix to the pan. Bring to the boil. Carefully lift the fish out of the pan and arrange on a warm serving plate, cover and keep warm.
7.   Continue to heat the sauce until reduced and thickened slightly. Taste and correct seasoning. Pour the sauce over the fish, sprinkle with the remaining parsley and garnish with lemon before serving.

HUNDRED HOUSE RED MULLET

HUNDRED HOUSE HOTEL
Norton, Shropshire

Henry, Sylvia & David Phillips with chef Anthony Baker

.

Red mullet, baked on a bed of fennel, leeks and mushrooms, with a tomato and basil sauce. Serve with mange tout or a crisp salad and new potatoes. To ease preparation, ask your fishmonger to prepare the red mullet for you, as detailed in the recipe.

Serves 4

4 × 150–200 g (6–8 oz) fresh red mullet
2 medium bulbs fennel
3 medium leeks
150 g (6 oz) mushrooms
seasoning
15 ml (1 tbsp) lemon juice
15 ml (1 tbsp) olive oil, plus a little for brushing
200 g (8 oz) ripe tomatoes
50 g (2 oz) fresh basil
150 g (6 oz) butter, softened

To serve:
a few feathery fennel leaves

1.   Scale, remove heads, gut and rinse the fish. Cut along both sides of the backbone to within 1.25 cm (½ inch) of the tail. Using scissors, cut through the backbone and carefully pull from the fish. Tweezer out any remaining large lateral bones, leaving the fish shape intact, joined by the tail.
2.   Preheat the oven to 200°C (400°F) mark 6.
3.   Cut the fennel, leeks and mushrooms into thin strips. Place the fennel in a saucepan with seasoning, lemon juice and olive oil. Fry for 2 minutes, then add the leeks and after 1 minute add the mushroom strips.
4.   On a baking tray, make 4 round flat beds with the fennel mixture. Season the mullet and brush with a little olive oil. Place a fish on each fennel bed, opening the fish up so the skin rests on the fennel and the fish forms a 'V' shape.
5.   Bake in the preheated oven for 30–40 minutes until just cooked.
6.   Liquidise and sieve the tomatoes. Bring the resulting liquid to the boil in a saucepan, add the basil leaves and leave to infuse over a very low flame for 10 minutes. Season and whisk in two thirds of the butter, cut into small knobs, with a balloon whisk.

7. Sieve the sauce and correct its consistency, whisking in more butter if too thin, or adding a little water or white wine if too thick. Check seasoning and keep warm until ready to serve but do not boil.
8. Lift the fish with its leek bed from the baking sheet, using a wide fish slice or spatula, and position on warmed serving plates. Flood the plate around the fish with sauce and garnish with fennel leaves.

SCRUMPY SOLE

THE KITCHEN
Polperro, Cornwall

Ian & Vanessa Bateson
.

Sole poached with onions and cider with a crispy cheese and breadcrumb crust. Serve with glazed carrot sticks and sautéed or chipped potatoes.

Serves 4

500 g (1 lb) onions, finely diced
30 ml (2 tbsp) olive oil
butter for greasing
4 large fillets sole, skinned
200 ml (8 fl oz) cider
15 ml (1 tbsp) lemon juice
15 ml (1 tbsp) chopped parsley
seasoning
50 g (2 oz) Cheddar cheese, grated
60 ml (4 tbsp) breadcrumbs

To serve:
1 lemon, cut into wedges

1. In a saucepan, heat the onions and oil together over a low heat for 12–15 minutes until the onions turn soft and brown.
2. Preheat the oven to 180°C (350°F) mark 4.
3. Butter an ovenproof dish or baking tray and spread the fillets, in a single layer, over the base. Pour the cider and lemon juice over the fish, spoon over the onions and sprinkle with parsley and seasoning. Scatter the cheese and breadcrumbs over the fish in an even layer.
4. Bake in the preheated oven for 12 minutes, then flash under a hot grill until the topping is crisp and golden.
5. Carefully transfer the fish to serving plates, using a wide fish slice or spatula, and spoon any cider sauce left in the baking tray over the top. Serve immediately, garnished with lemon wedges.

CHAMPAGNE DOVER SOLE

MON BIJOU
Bournemouth, Dorset

Di & John Bishop with chef Philip Nicholls

Fillets of Dover or lemon sole, rolled around layers of spinach and a delicate salmon mousse. Serve with a mixed salad.

Serves 4

12 large spinach leaves
4 × 200 g (8 oz) fresh Dover or lemon sole fillets, skinned
150 ml (6 fl oz) champagne

For the mousse:
200 g (8 oz) salmon
1 egg white
125 ml (5 fl oz) double cream
5 ml (1 tsp) lemon juice
seasoning

For the sauce:
25 g (1 oz) butter
15 g (½ oz) flour
375 ml (15 fl oz) fish stock (see page 200)
seasoning
30 ml (2 tbsp) double cream
15 ml (1 tbsp) tomato purée

To serve:
sprigs of fresh herbs

1.   Preheat the oven to 180°C (350°F) mark 4.
2.   Remove the stalks from the spinach and blanch in boiling water (1 minute), drain the leaves and spread out to dry on a clean tea towel.
3.   Prepare the salmon mousse. Making sure all the ingredients are cold to guarantee success, purée the salmon in the liquidiser with the egg white until smooth. Chill thoroughly, then beat in the double cream. Add the lemon juice and season.
4.   Place a spinach leaf over the skin side of each sole fillet and spread with salmon mousse. Carefully roll up the fillets and place in a lightly buttered ovenproof dish. Pour the champagne over the fish, cover and cook in the preheated oven for 20 minutes.
5.   Meanwhile, prepare the sauce. Melt the butter in a saucepan, stir in the flour to form a roux and cook for 2 minutes until sandy in texture. Gradually stir in the stock to form a smooth sauce, bring to the

boil then lower the heat and allow to simmer gently for 10 minutes. Season and stir in the cream.

6.   When the fish is cooked, drain the juice from the fish and add to the sauce. Keep the fish covered and warm until ready to serve.

7.   Stir the tomato purée into the sauce and bring to the boil. Taste and adjust seasoning, then simmer for 5–10 minutes, until reduced.

8.   Flood warmed dinner plates with the sauce. Carefully slice each fillet of sole into 4 and arrange in a semi-circle over the sauce to show off the spinach and mousse layers. Garnish with herbs and serve.

ROAST MONKFISH ELTON STYLE

ELTON HOTEL
Bramley, South Yorkshire
Peter & Wyna Keary with chef Gary Tune

Individual foil parcels of monkfish, baked with asparagus, chervil, Chablis and lemon juice. Serve with broccoli florets or a crisp green salad and lime-scented rice (see page 149).

Serves 6

750 g (1½ lb) monkfish, skinned
150 g (6 oz) tender, fresh asparagus
seasoning
100 g (4 oz) chopped fresh chervil
50 ml (2 fl oz) Chablis or other dry white wine
juice of ½ lemon

1.   Preheat the oven to 180°C (350°F) mark 4.

2.   Cut 6 × 30 cm (12 inch) squares of tin foil. Curl up the edges slightly to form a dip and arrange in a roasting tin.

3.   Cut the monkfish into chunks, divide between the foil packets.

4.   Blanch the asparagus in boiling salted water for 2 minutes, refresh under cold water and drain. Slice into 2.5 cm (1 inch) pieces and sprinkle over the monkfish.

5.   Season each of the packets, sprinkle with chervil and pour Chablis and lemon juice over each.

6.   Roll up the edges of the foil to create completely sealed parcels.

7.   Bake the parcels in the preheated oven for 15–20 minutes until the monkfish is bright white and cooked through.

8.   Place a foil packet on each dinner plate, leaving guests to open their own parcel and get the full benefit of the wonderful aroma.

CASSOULET OF MONKFISH

SEA COW RESTAURANT
Weymouth, Dorset

Terry Woolcock

•

A fish stew of monkfish, scallops, mussels, prawns, ginger, peppers and beansprouts. Serve in deep plates or bowls with a tossed salad and French bread.

Serves 4

25 g (1 oz) butter
1 clove garlic, crushed
15 g (½ oz) chopped parsley
300 g (12 oz) monkfish, trimmed and cut into fingers
8 scallops
250 ml (10 fl oz) Chablis
juice of 1 lemon
25 g (1 oz) fresh root ginger, chopped
125 ml (5 fl oz) ginger syrup (from a jar of preserved ginger)
50 g (2 oz) spring onions, chopped
50 g (2 oz) beansprouts
75 g (3 oz) mixed red and green peppers, cut into strips
7.5 g (¼ oz) chopped fresh dill
24 mussels, cleaned
seasoning
150 g (6 oz) prawns

1. Melt the butter with garlic and parsley in a large frying pan or saucepan. Add the monkfish and scallops and fry for 2 minutes. Remove the fish with a slotted spoon and keep to one side.
2. Add the Chablis, lemon juice, ginger, ginger syrup, spring onions, beansprouts, peppers, dill, mussels and seasoning to the pan, stir and as soon as the mussels open add the prawns.
3. Slice the scallops if they are very large and return with the monkfish to the pan.
4. Cook gently until the cooking liquid has reduced and thickened slightly, taking care not to overcook the fish. Taste and correct the seasoning and serve.

MONKFISH EILEAN IARMAIN

HOTEL EILEAN IARMAIN
Eilean Iarmain, Isle of Skye

Iain Noble

.

Slices of monkfish in a cream and bacon sauce. Serve with steamed broccoli spears topped with toasted almonds and buttered noodles or lime-scented rice (see page 149).

Serves 4

50 g (2 oz) butter
8 thin fillets monkfish
4 rashers bacon, diced
1 large onion, chopped
2 cloves garlic, crushed
juice of 2 lemons
2 bay leaves
2 sprigs fresh thyme
10 ml (2 tsp) chopped parsley
seasoning
200 ml (8 fl oz) white wine
300 ml (12 fl oz) double cream
2 egg yolks

To serve:
chopped parsley

1.   Melt the butter in a frying pan and gently fry the monkfish for 1 minute on each side. Add bacon, onion, garlic, lemon juice, bay leaves, thyme, parsley and seasoning and cook for 10 minutes, until the onion is transparent and the bacon cooked through.
2.   Using a spatula or slotted spoon, remove the fish from the pan and arrange on a warmed serving plate, cover and keep warm.
3.   Add the wine to the sauce, simmer for 1 minute, then stir in the cream. Take the pan off the heat and whisk in the egg yolks with a balloon whisk.
4.   Pour the sauce over the monkfish, sprinkle with chopped parsley and serve immediately.

Brochettes of Monkfish & Bacon with Lemon Sauce

FROGGIES WINE BAR AND RESTAURANT
Knaphill, Surrey

Robin & Debbie de Winton

.

Kebabs of marinated monkfish, with a creamy lemon sauce. Serve with crisp cooked mange tout and wild, brown or white rice.

Serves 6

1 kg (2 lb) monkfish tail, skinned and boned
12 rashers streaky bacon, rind removed
12 bay leaves (fresh if possible)
2 Spanish onions, peeled, quartered and torn into individual petals

For the marinade:
150 ml (6 fl oz) olive oil
1 clove garlic, crushed
juice and grated zest of 1 lemon
freshly ground black pepper

For the sauce:
3 egg yolks
juice and grated zest of 1 lemon
100 g (4 oz) butter
seasoning

1.   Cut the monkfish into 36 even-sized chunks.
2.   Cut each rasher of bacon into 3 and wrap 1 piece around each chunk of fish. Thread onto 6 bamboo or metal kebab skewers, using 6 chunks of bacon-wrapped monkfish, 2 bay leaves, and 6 onion petals per skewer. Arrange the brochettes in a shallow dish.
3.   In a bowl, whisk together all the marinade ingredients, pour over the brochettes and cover. Refrigerate for at least 4 hours.
4.   Preheat the oven to 220°C (425°F) mark 7.
5.   Line a baking sheet with foil and arrange the brochettes on top, leaving a space between each skewer. Bake at the top of the hot oven for 10–15 minutes, until the fish is white and the bacon crispy.
6.   While the brochettes are baking, prepare the sauce. Place the egg yolks, lemon juice, zest and half the butter in a double boiler or basin set over a pan of boiling water. Whisk until the sauce begins to thicken, then beat in the remaining butter, cut into pieces. Season.
7.   Set the brochettes on a bed of rice, spoon over sauce and serve.

CORNISH CRAB IN FILO PASTRY BAGS

THE KITCHEN
Polperro, Cornwall

Ian & Vanessa Bateson

.

Hot filo pastry bags, filled with white crab meat, set on a tomato, cream and basil sauce. Serve with a light mixed salad.

Serves 4

4 sheets filo pastry
25 g (1 oz) butter, melted
300 g (12 oz) white crab meat

For the sauce:
8 medium tomatoes
100 ml (4 fl oz) double cream
16 large basil leaves, chopped
seasoning

1. Preheat the oven to 180°C (350°F) mark 4.
2. Working quickly, so the pastry doesn't dry out, cut the filo pastry sheets into 16 strips approximately 30 × 10 cm (12 × 4 inches). Take 4 strips and cover the remaining sheets with a damp tea towel.
3. Set out the first 4 pastry strips so they form a star or 'spokes of a wheel' shape, crossing in the centre. Brush with melted butter. Place a tall mound of crab meat in the centre of the pastry. Pick up the ends of the top strip of pastry and pinch together over the crab, allowing the ends to curl out slightly like the petals of a rose above the join. Brush the outer side of the pastry strip with melted butter, then bring up the next piece of pastry, pinch over the crab and create the next layer of rose petals. Continue with the other 2 pastry strips and place the completed parcel on a baking tray while preparing the remaining 3 bags. The crab should be completely enclosed in the finished pastry parcel. Brush the outside of the parcels with melted butter.
4. Bake in the preheated oven for 15 minutes until the pastry is golden.
5. Prepare the sauce by liquidising and sieving the tomatoes. Place the resulting tomato liquid in a saucepan and bring to the boil. Add the cream and basil, stir until slightly thickened. Season to taste.
6. Flood the base of 4 dinner plates with the hot sauce and place a filo crab parcel in the centre of each. Serve immediately.

COQUILLES ST. JACQUES AU NOILLY

LES QUAT' SAISONS – 1977

Raymond Blanc

·

Scallops cooked in Noilly Prat. Prepare this recipe using only plump fresh scallops and firm white button mushrooms. To produce a more substantial dish, place a bed of blanched spinach or Swiss chard under the scallops before serving. This recipe was served as a fish course in Raymond Blanc's first restaurant – Les Quat' Saisons, Summertown, Oxford – which was Les Routiers recommended.

Serves 4

16 large fresh scallops, corals discarded
seasoning

For braising the scallops:
4 shallots, chopped
15 ml (1 tbsp) butter
100 g (4 oz) button mushrooms
200 ml (8 fl oz) Noilly Prat
100 ml (4 fl oz) fish stock (see page 200)

For the sauce:
200 ml (8 fl oz) double cream
100 g (4 oz) button mushrooms, sliced
2 egg yolks
juice of ¼ lemon
seasoning

1.　Cut the scallops in half widthways.
2.　Preheat the oven to 190°C (375°F) mark 5.
3.　Prepare the braising liquor. In a large flameproof casserole, sweat the shallots in the butter until soft but not coloured. Add the mushrooms and sweat for a further minute. Add the Noilly Prat and bring to the boil, simmer until reduced to half the volume, then add the fish stock.
4.　Season the scallops, then arrange them in a single layer in the pan with the braising liquid and partially cover with a lid. On the hob, bring to the boil, then place the pan in the preheated oven and bake for 6 minutes.
5.　Strain the braising juices into a second saucepan, cover the scallops and keep warm while preparing the sauce.

6.   Whip 125 ml (5 fl oz) of the cream until thick and keep to one side.
7.   Heat the strained scallop cooking liquor and simmer until reduced to half its volume. Pour in the remaining cream and add the sliced mushrooms. Remove the pan from the heat and allow to cool slightly. Using a balloon whisk, whisk the egg yolks into the sauce (if the sauce is too hot when the egg yolks are added it will curdle), followed by the lemon juice, seasoning and whipped cream.
8.   Preheat the grill.
9.   Arrange the cooked scallops on 4 warmed heatproof plates, spoon the sauce over the top and place under the hot grill for 30–40 seconds, until the sauce glistens. Serve.

Poached Jumbo Scallops Wrapped in Dover Sole

THE LORD NELSON & CARRIAGES RESTAURANT
Marshfield, Wiltshire

Roy & Jeanette Lane with chef Paul Cuss

·

Fillets of Dover sole rolled around scallops, served in a sherry and cream sauce flavoured with physallis (cape gooseberries) and white grapes, with a rice and grape tower. Serve with green beans or salad.

Serves 4

250 g (10 oz) cooked white rice
seasoning
125 g (5 oz) seedless white grapes
25 g (1 oz) butter, plus extra for greasing
25 g (1 oz) flour
400 ml (16 fl oz) good fish stock (see page 200)
1 punnet cape gooseberries (physallis)
8 large scallops
2 × 500 g (1 lb) Dover sole, skinned and filleted
1 onion, finely chopped
375 ml (15 fl oz) dry sherry
50 ml (2 fl oz) double cream

To serve:
chopped parsley

1.   Preheat the oven to 200°C (400°F) mark 6.
2.   In a bowl, season the cooked rice. Dice and stir in 25 g (1 oz) of the seedless grapes. Thoroughly butter 4 tea cups or ramekin dishes and pile the rice and grape mixture into them. Stand the ramekins in a roasting tin, half filled with boiling water, cover with foil and place in the hot oven for 15 minutes until warmed through.
3.   Meanwhile, prepare the sauce. Melt the butter in a saucepan, stir in the flour and gradually add all but 50 ml (2 fl oz) of the fish stock. Season and bring to the boil, then simmer, uncovered, for 3 minutes. Add the remaining grapes and cape gooseberries.
4.   Remove the coral-coloured roe from the scallops and reserve. Wrap a fillet of sole around each white scallop and secure with a cocktail stick.
5.   Lightly butter an earthenware casserole dish and sprinkle the base with chopped onion. Arrange the sole-wrapped scallops over the top and pour the remaining 50 ml (2 fl oz) fish stock and 75 ml (3 fl oz) of the sherry over the fish. Season, cover with a lid or buttered greaseproof paper and place in the hot oven for 10–15 minutes, until the fish is cooked through.
6.   While the fish is cooking, bring the remaining sherry and scallop coral to the boil in a saucepan. Simmer for 2 minutes, then drain, adding the cooking liquid to the sauce. Cover the coral and keep warm.
7.   Using a slotted spoon, carefully take the fish from the casserole, remove the cocktail sticks and arrange on a warm serving plate. Cover and keep warm. Strain the cooking liquid into the sauce and bring back to the boil. Stir in the cream, taste and correct seasoning.
8.   Carefully unmould a portion of rice onto each plate, arrange 2 scallop and sole rolls around the rice, top with a piece of cooked coral and spoon a little sauce, with some fruit, over the fish. Sprinkle with chopped parsley and serve, offering extra sauce in a jug.

SCALLOPS ST. DUBRICIUS

PENGETHLEY MANOR
Ross-on-Wye, Herefordshire
Patrick & Geraldine Wisker with chef Ferdinand Van Der Knaap

.

Scallops wrapped in vine leaves and braised in a wine, Bénédictine and fish sauce. Serve with a mixed salad and rice.

Serves 4

8 large vine leaves
1 large onion, finely chopped
1 clove garlic, crushed
6 large tomatoes, skinned and chopped
12 large scallops
seasoning
250 ml (10 fl oz) fish sauce (available from Oriental grocers)
150 ml (6 fl oz) white wine
15 ml (1 tbsp) Bénédictine
15 ml (1 tbsp) chopped parsley

1.   If the vine leaves are tough, blanch in boiling water for 2 minutes, then drain thoroughly.
2.   In a bowl, mix together the onion, garlic, tomatoes, scallops and seasoning. Divide this mixture between the vine leaves and roll up into tight parcels.
3.   Put the fish sauce, wine and Bénédictine into a saucepan and arrange the vine leaves in a single layer over the base. Heat the pan, allowing the liquid to simmer gently for 8 minutes.
4.   Remove the vine leaf parcels from the pan and arrange on a warmed serving dish. Sprinkle with the parsley.
5.   If you would like to serve a sauce with this dish, increase the heat under the cooking liquid and boil until reduced to half the volume. Serve in a warmed jug.

SEAFOOD LASAGNE

VICTORIA INN
West Marden, West Sussex
James Neville
.

Lasagne pasta, layered with monkfish, prawns and crab in tomato sauce, topped with a cheesy white sauce. Serve with garlic bread and a mixed green salad.

Serves 6–8

250 g (10 oz) lasagne pasta
butter for greasing

For the fish and tomato sauce:
25 g (1 oz) butter
1 small onion, finely chopped
2 cloves garlic, crushed
175 g (7 oz) monkfish tail, skinned and diced
15 ml (1 tbsp) tomato purée
either 1 × 397 g (14 oz) can of tomatoes
or 500 g (1 lb) tomatoes, skinned and chopped and 5 ml (1 tsp) tomato
purée
250 ml (10 fl oz) white wine
75 g (3 oz) white crab meat
175 g (7 oz) peeled prawns
45 ml (3 tbsp) chopped fresh basil
seasoning

For the white sauce:
25 g (1 oz) butter
25 g (1 oz) flour
500 ml (1 pint) milk
seasoning
75 g (3 oz) dark crab meat
175 g (7 oz) Mozzarella cheese, grated

For the topping:
45 ml (3 tbsp) grated Parmesan cheese

1. Preheat the oven to 200°C (400°F) mark 6.
2. First prepare the fish and tomato sauce. Melt the butter in a saucepan and fry the onion and garlic until softened. Add the monkfish and stir until sealed. Stir in the tomato purée and cook for 1 minute, then add tomatoes, white wine, white crab meat, prawns, basil and seasoning. Simmer for 1 minute.

3. Cook the pasta according to manufacturer's instructions, drain and keep in a basin of cold water to prevent it sticking together.
4. Meanwhile, cook the white sauce. Melt the butter, stir in the flour and gradually add the milk, heat until thickened slightly. Season and stir in the dark crab meat and Mozzarella.
5. Butter an ovenproof dish. Layer with lasagne pasta followed by fish and tomato sauce, white sauce and pasta until full, finishing with a layer of white sauce. Sprinkle the top with Parmesan and bake in the preheated oven for 30–40 minutes until piping hot and golden on top.

BAKED EYEMOUTH CRAB

THE OLD FORGE RESTAURANT
Newmill on Teviot, Borders

Bill & Margaret Irving

Hot crab in a mustard and yogurt sauce. Serve with steamed carrot sticks and minted potatoes.

Serves 6

50 g (2 oz) butter
100 g (4 oz) onion, chopped
500 g (1 lb) crab meat, both brown and white
20 ml (4 tsp) whole grain mustard
100 g (4 oz) fresh brown breadcrumbs
250 ml (10 fl oz) natural yogurt
seasoning
50 g (2 oz) Cheddar cheese, grated

To serve:
1 banana, sliced and dipped in lemon juice
6 sprigs of fresh dill

1. Preheat the oven to 220°C (425°F) mark 7.
2. Melt the butter in a saucepan and fry the onion for 5–8 minutes, until soft but not coloured.
3. Stir in the crab meat, mustard, breadcrumbs, yogurt and seasoning to taste.
4. Spoon the mixture into washed crab shells or large ramekin dishes and sprinkle with grated cheese. Bake in the preheated oven for 10–15 minutes until puffed-up and golden.
5. Arrange several slices of banana on top of each crab and garnish with the fresh dill. Serve immediately.

FRESH SEAFOOD PIE

OLD SCHOOL HOUSE
Kinlochbervie, Highland

Tom & Margaret Burt

·

A haddock and prawn fish pie, topped with cheesy potato. Serve with fresh, crisply-cooked vegetables.

Serves 4–6

500 g (1 lb) haddock fillets
1 bouquet garni
75 g (3 oz) butter
1 small onion, finely chopped
100 g (4 oz) mushrooms
40 g (1½ oz) flour
250 ml (10 fl oz) milk
125 ml (5 fl oz) chicken stock
100 g (4 oz) Cheddar cheese, grated
100 g (4 oz) fresh prawns, peeled
15 ml (1 tbsp) chopped parsley
3 hard-boiled eggs, peeled and chopped
5 ml (1 tsp) lemon juice
seasoning

For the topping:
2 large potatoes, peeled and cooked
15 ml (1 tbsp) milk
50 g (2 oz) butter
25 g (1 oz) Cheddar cheese, grated

1. Poach the haddock with 60 ml (4 tbsp) water and the bouquet garni for 8 minutes. Drain, saving the fish stock. Skin and flake the fish.
2. Melt the butter for the pie in a large saucepan. Add the onion and fry for 3 minutes, then add the mushrooms and continue to cook, stirring, for 2 minutes. Stir in the flour and cook for 1 minute, then add the milk and chicken stock. Add the cheese, prawns, half the parsley, the haddock, eggs, lemon juice and seasoning. Bring to the boil.
3. Add some, or all, of the reserved fish stock, keeping the sauce relatively thick. Taste and correct seasoning. Pour into a warm pie dish.
4. Mash the cooked potatoes with the milk and half the butter, season and stir in the cheese. Pipe or spoon the potato onto the top of the pie and dot with the remaining butter. Cook under a hot grill for 5–10 minutes until browned. Sprinkle with remaining parsley and serve.

SPICY CREOLE-STYLE FISH PIE

THE CROWN INN
Arford, Hampshire

Colin & Jane Greenhalgh

.

Coley in a piquant tomato and pepper sauce, topped with a puff pastry lid. Serve with sautéed courgettes and creamed sweetcorn.

Serves 4

500 g (1 lb) coley, skinned
500 ml (1 pint) milk
1 bay leaf
bouquet garni
2 carrots, peeled
1 onion, quartered
6 black peppercorns
30 ml (2 tbsp) olive oil
1 red pepper, diced
1 green pepper, diced
10 ml (2 tsp) curry powder
5 ml (1 tsp) chilli powder
100 g (4 oz) tomatoes, skinned and chopped
15 ml (1 tbsp) tomato purée
seasoning
300–500 g (12–16 oz) puff pastry
milk to glaze

1.   Preheat the oven to 220°C (425°F) mark 7.
2.   Place the coley, milk, bay leaf, bouquet garni, whole carrots, onion and black peppercorns together in a saucepan. Bring the liquid to the boil and simmer gently for 15–20 minutes until the fish is just tender. Remove the pan from the heat and leave to cool.
3.   While the fish is cooking, heat the oil in a separate saucepan and fry the peppers for 5 minutes until softened. Add the curry and chilli powders; if you like very spicy food, use slightly more than the given quantity. Stir in the tomatoes, tomato purée and seasoning. Bring to the boil, then simmer for 5 minutes. Taste and correct seasoning.
4.   Lightly butter a pie dish. Strain the coley, reserving the stock. Roughly flake the coley into the pie dish, keeping the chunks large.
5.   Pour the tomato sauce over the fish and add enough of the reserved cooking liquid just to cover the fish with sauce. Allow to cool.
6.   On a lightly floured surface, roll out the pastry and cover the pie. Decorate the top with pastry trimmings. Brush the pastry with a little milk and bake in the preheated oven for 25–30 minutes.

AUBERGINE BAKE

THE GEORGE INN
Cambridge, Gloucestershire
Alistair & Jane Deas with chef Josephine Nelmes

·

Layers of aubergine, cheese and hard-boiled egg, baked in a tomato sauce, with a crisp cheese and breadcrumb topping. Serve with a green salad or set on top of savoury rice.

Serves 4

3 medium aubergines
salt
butter for frying and greasing
2 eggs, lightly beaten
either 1 × 397 g (14 oz) can of tomatoes
or 500 g (1 lb) tomatoes, skinned and chopped and 5 ml (1 tsp) tomato purée
1 large onion, chopped
2 cloves garlic, crushed
seasoning
200 g (8 oz) Gruyère cheese, thinly sliced
4 hard-boiled eggs, peeled and sliced (optional)
50 g (2 oz) breadcrumbs
200 g (8 oz) Cheddar cheese, grated
2 tomatoes, sliced
5 ml (1 tsp) paprika

1.   Cut the aubergines into slices, sprinkle liberally with salt and leave to drain in a colander for 30 minutes. Wash off the salt.
2.   Heat some butter in a frying pan, dip the aubergine slices in the beaten eggs and fry in the hot fat until slightly browned on both sides. Drain on kitchen paper.
3.   In a saucepan, heat together the tomatoes, onion and garlic, season and simmer for 10 minutes.
4.   Preheat the oven to 180°C (350°F) mark 4.
5.   Grease an ovenproof baking dish. Fill with the bake ingredients in layers; aubergine slices, Gruyère, hard-boiled egg, until the dish is nearly full. Pour the tomato sauce over the top and leave for several minutes to allow the sauce to filter through the dish.
6.   Mix the breadcrumbs and grated cheese together and sprinkle in an even layer over the top. Garnish with the tomato slices and paprika.
7.   Bake in the preheated oven for 40 minutes, or until the topping is crisp and golden brown.

RED DRAGON BAKE

ROSE & CROWN INN
Snettisham, Norfolk

Margaret Trafford

A potato-topped bean and grain pie. Serve with a crunchy side salad.

Serves 4

150 g (6 oz) aduki beans
100 g (4 oz) wheat grain or nutty brown rice
15 ml (1 tbsp) olive oil
2 onions, peeled and chopped
1 clove garlic, crushed
250 g (10 oz) carrots, scrubbed and diced
15–30 ml (1–2 tbsp) soy sauce
30 ml (2 tbsp) tomato purée
5 ml (1 tsp) mixed herbs
seasoning
butter for greasing

For the topping:
500 g (1 lb) potatoes, peeled and boiled
50 g (2 oz) butter
pinch of grated nutmeg
seasoning

1. Wash the aduki beans and wheat grain or rice and soak overnight. Alternatively, steep the beans and grain in boiling water for 1 hour.
2. Drain the beans and grain. Cover with water in a saucepan and boil for 30 minutes until the beans are just softened. Drain, reserving the cooking liquid.
3. Heat the oil in a pan, fry the onions and garlic for 5 minutes. Add the carrots and cook for 2–3 minutes. Add the beans and grains.
4. Add the soy sauce, tomato purée, herbs and 375 ml (15 fl oz) of the reserved bean cooking liquid to the saucepan. Bring to the boil and simmer for 20–30 minutes until the flavours are well blended. Season and add a little more bean liquid to the pan if necessary.
5. Pour the bean stew into a lightly greased casserole dish.
6. Preheat the oven to 180°C (350°F) mark 4.
7. For the topping, mash the cooked potato with half the butter, the nutmeg and seasoning to taste. Spread over the top of the casserole and dot with the remaining butter.
8. Bake in the preheated oven for 35–40 minutes until the casserole is heated through and the top is brown and crunchy.

NUTTY MARROW BAKE

LONG'S RESTAURANT
Truro, Cornwall

Ian & Ann Long

.

Marrow filled with a nutty stuffing, baked in white wine, topped with crisp croûtons and served with a sauce of yellow pepper purée. Serve with crisply cooked carrots and French beans or follow with a salad tossed in Stilton dressing. The stuffing mixture used in this recipe could make a meal on its own. Bake in a lightly buttered dish, turn out and serve with a sherry and cream sauce.

Serves 4

1 medium marrow
butter for greasing
125 ml (5 fl oz) white wine

For the croûtons:
day-old brown bread
oil for frying

For the stuffing:
15 g (½ oz) butter
4 sticks celery, cubed
1 onion, very finely chopped
5 ml (1 tsp) yeast extract
150 g (6 oz) button mushrooms, thinly sliced
½ avocado, peeled and cubed
2 small or 1 large tomato, skinned, seeded and sliced
100 g (4 oz) mixed nuts, roughly chopped (not too many walnuts as they can overpower the flavour and be slightly bitter)
5 ml (1 tsp) mixed herbs
50 g (2 oz) brown breadcrumbs
seasoning
1 egg, beaten

For the yellow pepper purée:
3 yellow peppers
½ onion
25 g (1 oz) butter
65 ml (2½ fl oz) medium sherry
seasoning

1. For the croûtons, cut the stale bread into 1.25 cm (½ inch) cubes and fry in the oil until golden. Drain thoroughly, then store in an airtight tin until required.

2. Prepare all the stuffing ingredients. Melt the butter in a frying pan, add the celery and onion and cook until soft. Turn into a mixing bowl and stir in the yeast extract, mushrooms, avocado, tomato, nuts, herbs and breadcrumbs. Taste for seasoning and fold in the beaten egg.

3. Preheat the oven to 180°C (350°F) mark 4.

4. Peel the marrow, cut in half lengthwise and, using a metal spoon, scoop out the seeds. Cook the marrow in a large saucepan of boiling water for 2–3 minutes to soften the flesh, remove from the pan and drain thoroughly on kitchen paper.

5. Fill the marrow cavity with stuffing, moulding so the other half can be replaced over the filling. Tie the marrow together with tape or string so it keeps its shape. Butter a small casserole dish and fill with stuffing mix not used in the marrow, cover and cook alongside the marrow.

6. Butter a roasting tin and place the prepared marrow inside. Pour the wine over the top, cover with greaseproof paper and foil and bake in the hot oven for 25 minutes.

7. Remove the paper and foil, spoon some cooking liquid over the marrow and return to cook for a further 30 minutes until the marrow is tender, basting occasionally.

8. Prepare the pepper purée while the marrow is cooking. Cut the peppers in half, remove the seeds and pith, then slice into even-sized cubes.

9. Cut the onion into pieces approximately the same size as the peppers to ensure even cooking.

10. Melt the butter in a saucepan, cook the onion for 2 minutes, add the peppers and pour in the sherry. Stir together, cover with a sheet of greaseproof paper and place a lid on the saucepan. Turn the heat down as low as possible and cook for 30 minutes until both the onions and peppers are tender.

11. In a blender, liquidise the pepper mixture to a purée, then push through a sieve with the help of a wooden spoon. Taste and season.

12. When the marrow is cooked, remove from the oven. Strain the cooking liquid into a saucepan, bring to the boil and simmer until reduced to half volume. Meanwhile, keep the marrow covered and warm.

13. Add the pepper purée to the reduced cooking liquid, taste and correct seasoning.

14. Untie the marrow and cut into portions.

15. Flood the base of 4 warmed plates with the pepper sauce, arrange a slice of the marrow on top, together with a spoonful of extra stuffing mix, and sprinkle with the crisp croûtons. Serve immediately, offering the remaining pepper sauce in a jug.

HERB PANCAKES WITH SPINACH & NUTS

THE CROWN OF CRUCIS
Ampney Crucis, Gloucestershire

Mr R.K. Mills

.

Pancakes filled with a mixture of spinach and chopped nuts in a creamy herb sauce. Serve with baked tomatoes and a salad or fresh granary bread. If time is limited, buy a pack of 8 pancakes, now available ready made in most large supermarkets, rather than preparing your own. If you prefer a moist pancake, prepare 500 ml (1 pint) of cheese sauce and pour over the pancakes before baking.

Serves 4

For the pancakes:
100 g (4 oz) flour
pinch of salt
1 egg, lightly beaten
250 ml (10 fl oz) milk
15 ml (1 tbsp) chopped mixed fresh herbs
lard for frying

For the filling:
1 onion, peeled and sliced finely
1 clove garlic, crushed
100 g (4 oz) mushrooms, sliced
25 g (1 oz) butter
100 g (4 oz) hazelnuts, chopped in the food processor
50 g (2 oz) mixed nuts, chopped in the food processor
500 g (1 lb) frozen spinach, thawed
10 ml (2 tsp) mixed herbs
pinch of grated nutmeg
10 ml (2 tsp) Worcestershire Sauce
10 ml (2 tsp) lemon juice
seasoning
125 ml (5 fl oz) single cream
butter for greasing
75 g (3 oz) Cheddar cheese, grated
pinch of paprika

To serve:
chopped parsley

1.   Prepare the pancakes if making at home. Sift the flour and salt into a large bowl, pour the beaten egg into the centre, then pour in half the milk, gradually working the flour into the egg and milk with a wooden spoon. Whisk until the mixture is completely lump free, allow to stand for 2 minutes, then stir in the remaining milk, beating until the batter has the consistency of single cream. Add the chopped fresh herbs to the batter.
2.   Melt the lard in a frying pan. When very hot, cook the pancakes – you should get between 8 and 10 from this mixture. Pile up, with a sheet of greaseproof paper between each pancake.
3.   Now prepare the filling by frying the onion, garlic and mushrooms in half the butter until softened. Stir in the nuts, add the spinach, mixed herbs, nutmeg, Worcestershire Sauce, lemon juice and seasoning. Cook over a low heat for 5 minutes.
4.   Stir in the cream and remaining butter, taste and correct seasoning, then allow the mixture to cool.
5.   Assemble the pancakes. Place a couple of spoonfuls of filling inside each pancake, roll up and arrange in a greased ovenproof dish. Cover with grated cheese and a sprinkling of paprika. Place under the grill, or in a hot oven, for 15 minutes, until the pancakes are heated through and the cheese topping has melted. Serve immediately, sprinkled with chopped parsley.

PENSCOT VEGETARIAN NUT ROAST

PENSCOT FARMHOUSE HOTEL
Winscombe, Somerset

Tony & Karen Tilden with chef Malcolm Harwood

·

A peanut, onion, tomato, apple and herb loaf. Serve with home-made hot tomato sauce, green vegetables or salad.

Serves 4

polyunsaturated oil for greasing
200 g (8 oz) raw peanuts, brown outer skin removed
50 g (2 oz) vegetable margarine
2 onions, finely sliced
1 large tomato, skinned and chopped
2 small dessert apples, peeled and diced
25 g (1 oz) oatmeal
5 ml (1 tsp) chopped sage
seasoning
1 egg
little milk

1. Preheat the oven to 180°C (350°F) mark 4. Grease a 500 g (1 lb) loaf tin.
2. Chop, mince or grind the peanuts.
3. Heat the margarine in a frying pan, add the onions, tomato and apples. Fry for 10 minutes until the onion has softened. Stir in the peanuts, oatmeal, sage and seasoning.
4. Away from the heat, stir in the egg and enough milk to give a fairly moist consistency.
5. Press the mixture into the prepared tin, spreading the top level. Cover with greased foil and bake in the preheated oven for 1 hour or until springy to the touch.
6. Turn the cooked loaf out of the tin, garnish and serve.

SPICY RED BEAN & BULGAR WHEAT STEW

HENLEY HOTEL
Bigbury-on-Sea, Devon

Mrs L. Beer

.

A spicy kidney bean stew. Serve spooned over rice or a jacket potato.

Serves 4

200 g (8 oz) red kidney beans, soaked overnight
1 large onion, chopped
2 cloves garlic, crushed
30 ml (2 tbsp) olive oil
2 carrots, chopped
2 sticks celery, chopped
1 green pepper, chopped
2.5 ml (½ tsp) chilli powder
1.25 ml (¼ tsp) cayenne pepper
2.5 ml (½ tsp) fenugreek, ground
5 ml (1 tsp) cumin
10 ml (2 tsp) coriander
either 1 × 397 g (14 oz) can of tomatoes
or 500 g (1 lb) tomatoes, skinned and chopped and 5 ml (1 tsp) tomato
purée
45 ml (3 tbsp) tomato purée
5 ml (1 tsp) caster sugar
75 g (3 oz) bulgar wheat
seasoning

To serve:
soured cream

1. Boil the soaked kidney beans rapidly in water for 10 minutes, reduce the heat and simmer for 30–40 minutes until soft.
2. Heat the onion, garlic and oil together in a large saucepan, stir and cook for 3 minutes until the onion has started to soften. Add the carrots, celery, pepper and spices to the pan, stir and continue to cook for 5–8 minutes until the onion is transparent.
3. Drain the cooked kidney beans, saving 500 ml (1 pint) of the cooking liquid. Add the beans to the vegetable saucepan, then stir in all the remaining ingredients, including the reserved bean cooking liquid.
4. Bring to the boil and allow to simmer for 30–40 minutes, stirring occasionally, until the bulgar wheat is cooked. Taste and correct seasoning before serving, accompanied by a bowl of soured cream.

FRESH VEGETABLE BAKE PROVENÇALE

LE BISTRO
Wirksworth, Derbyshire

Mark Fox

.

Fresh vegetables baked in a puff pastry parcel, set on a provençale sauce. Serve with hot garlic bread.

Serves 6

For the parcels:
25 g (1 oz) butter
15 ml (1 tbsp) olive oil
1 onion, chopped
1 clove garlic, crushed
1 green pepper, chopped
1 carrot, peeled and diced
1 stick celery, sliced
10 ml (2 tsp) cumin, ground
10 ml (2 tsp) coriander seeds, ground
seasoning
100 g (4 oz) mixed fresh seasonal vegetables, diced (cauliflower, green beans, asparagus, broccoli, baby corn or courgettes, for example)
100 g (4 oz) mushrooms, sliced
300 g (12 oz) puff pastry
1 egg, lightly beaten
butter for greasing

For the sauce:
1 kg (2 lb) ripe tomatoes, skinned
30 ml (2 tbsp) olive oil
1 large onion, finely chopped
2 cloves garlic, crushed
generous pinch of dried basil
5 ml (1 tsp) chopped rosemary
1 bay leaf
bouquet garni
15 ml (1 tbsp) tomato purée
5 ml (1 tsp) caster sugar
250 ml (10 fl oz) water or red wine
seasoning

To serve:
sprigs of coriander

1. Preheat the oven to 220°C (425°F) mark 7.
2. First prepare the parcels. Heat the butter and oil together in a large saucepan. Fry the onion, garlic, green pepper, carrot and celery together for 5 minutes, until the onion is transparent. Add the cumin, coriander and seasoning, turn off the heat and keep to one side.
3. In a steamer or colander, set over a pan of boiling water, gently steam the mixed vegetables until just softened. Add these vegetables to the onion mixture, along with the sliced mushrooms.
4. On a lightly floured surface, roll out the pastry until fairly thin and cut into 6 large or 12 small equal squares. Divide the vegetable filling between the pastry squares, moisten the edges with beaten egg, then fold the pastry to form completely enclosed parcels. Pinch the joining seams together and decorate the top with pastry trimmings. Arrange the parcels on a lightly greased baking sheet and brush with beaten egg. Bake in the preheated oven for 30–35 minutes until risen and golden.
5. Meanwhile, for the sauce, cut the skinned tomatoes in half and chop roughly.
6. Heat the oil in a saucepan and cook the onion and garlic over a low heat for 10 minutes. Add the chopped tomatoes, basil, rosemary, bay leaf, bouquet garni, tomato purée, sugar, water and seasoning. Stir and allow to simmer for 20–30 minutes until reduced to a pungent, thick sauce. Remove the bay leaf and bouquet garni. If you prefer a smooth sauce, liquidise and pass through a fine sieve at this point, then reheat.
7. Cover the base of 6 warmed dinner plates with hot provençale sauce, place 1 large or 2 small vegetable parcels in the centre of each and garnish with sprigs of fresh coriander. Serve immediately.

FETTUCCINE WITH NUTS & MUSHROOMS

OLD SWAN INN
Llantwit Major, South Glamorgan
Geoff & Myra Radford
·

Ribbon pasta in a creamy, nut and mushroom sauce. Serve with a crunchy salad and hunks of fresh bread. If you are unable to buy fettuccine use tagliatelle.

Serves 8 as a starter, 4 as a main course

150 g (6 oz) mixed nuts, roughly chopped (walnuts, hazelnuts, almonds and cashew nuts, for example)
50 g (2 oz) butter
25 g (1 oz) flour
500 ml (1 pint) milk
1 bay leaf
seasoning
200 g (8 oz) mushrooms, chopped
500 g (1 lb) fresh fettuccine or 250 g (10 oz) dried pasta
30 ml (2 tbsp) single cream
25 g (1 oz) flaked almonds
25 g (1 oz) chopped parsley

To serve:
freshly grated Parmesan cheese

1. Boil the chopped mixed nuts in a pan of water for about 20 minutes until slightly soft, then drain thoroughly.
2. Melt two thirds of the butter in a saucepan, stir in the flour then gradually add the milk to form a smooth white sauce. Add the bay leaf and season liberally. Stir the drained nuts into the sauce.
3. Melt the remaining butter in a separate saucepan and gently fry the mushrooms until softened. Stir into the white sauce.
4. In a large pan of boiling, salted water, cook the fettuccine until just soft, drain.
5. Gently reheat the nut sauce then remove the bay leaf and stir in the cream. In a large warm pasta bowl or saucepan, toss the fettuccine in the sauce until evenly coated. Divide between individual serving dishes, sprinkle with almonds and parsley and serve immediately with a bowl of Parmesan cheese.

PENNE BROCCOLI

LA BUCA
York, North Yorkshire
Geoff Gracey with chef Nicola Tragni

.

Pasta with an anchovy, broccoli, bacon and chilli sauce. Serve with a mixed or tomato and basil salad. If you do not like anchovies, omit them and increase the quantity of bacon.

Serves 4–6

500 g (1 lb) broccoli
500 g (1 lb) penne – tube-shaped pasta pieces
50 g (2 oz) virgin olive oil
2 cloves garlic, crushed
25 g (1 oz) anchovies
1 medium fresh green chilli, chopped
2 slices white bread, cut into small dice
3 rashers lean bacon
15 ml (1 tbsp) chopped parsley
black pepper

To serve:
freshly grated Parmesan cheese

1.   Cut the broccoli into bite-sized florets. Cook the pasta in plenty of boiling, salted water, adding the broccoli to the water for the last 3–4 minutes of cooking (depending on how well cooked you like broccoli). Drain thoroughly and turn into a large warmed pasta bowl or serving dish. Cover to keep warm.
2.   While the pasta is cooking, heat the olive oil in a frying pan and add the garlic, anchovies, chilli, bread, bacon and parsley. Fry for 3–5 minutes, stirring constantly until the bread is golden and the bacon cooked.
3.   Pour the contents of the frying pan over the pasta and broccoli, liberally grate black pepper over the dish and toss to mix the pasta and sauce thoroughly. Serve immediately, accompanied by a bowl of Parmesan cheese.

VEGETARIAN GOULASH

ROSE & CROWN INN
Snettisham, Norfolk
Margaret Trafford

.

A spicy vegetable stew. Serve in deep bowls with crusty bread or set on a bed of rice. Vary the vegetables used in the goulash according to seasonal availability – celery, green beans, leeks or mushrooms could all be used.

Serves 4

30 ml (2 tbsp) olive oil
2 onions, peeled and chopped
10 ml (2 tsp) wholemeal flour
10 ml (2 tsp) Hungarian paprika
pinch of cayenne
seasoning
either 1 × 397 g (14 oz) can of tomatoes
or 500 g (1 lb) tomatoes, peeled and chopped and 5 ml (1 tsp) tomato purée
5 ml (1 tsp) tomato purée
250 ml (10 fl oz) hot water
200 g (8 oz) cauliflower, cut into sprigs
200 g (8 oz) new carrots, peeled and cut into chunks
200 g (8 oz) courgettes, cut into chunks
200 g (8 oz) small new potatoes, washed and halved
½ green pepper, chopped
125 ml (5 fl oz) soured cream or yogurt

1.   Preheat the oven to 180°C (350°F) mark 4.
2.   Heat the oil in a flameproof casserole dish and fry the onions for 5–6 minutes until softened. Stir in the flour, most of the paprika, cayenne pepper and seasoning. Cook for 1 minute.
3.   Stir in the tomatoes, tomato purée and water and bring the sauce to the boil, stirring constantly.
4.   Add the vegetables, taste and adjust seasoning and paprika levels.
5.   Cover and bake in the hot oven for 30–40 minutes until the vegetables are just softened. Serve while piping hot, topped with a spoonful of soured cream or yogurt.

Summer Profiteroles (page 178)

MEDITERRANEAN OKRA

THE RESTAURANT ON THE GREEN
Richmond, North Yorkshire

Alan & Helen Bennett

.

Okra baked in tomato sauce. Serve as a vegetarian pasta sauce, or as a meal on its own, set in a deep bowl with a hunk of fresh wholemeal bread.

Serves 8 as a starter, 4 as a main course

500 g (1 lb) okra
2 onions, chopped
2 cloves garlic, crushed
60 ml (4 tbsp) olive oil
12 ripe tomatoes, skinned
2 bay leaves
250 ml (10 fl oz) water
seasoning

To serve:
chopped parsley

1.   Slice the thick stalk ends from the okra, wash and drain.
2.   In a saucepan, fry the onion and garlic in the oil for 5 minutes until soft and transparent.
3.   Rough chop the skinned tomatoes and add to the onion with the bay leaves and water. Bring to the boil and allow to simmer for 5 minutes.
4.   Add the okra to the pan and continue to simmer for 5 minutes until the okra is tender, adding a little more water if necessary. Season to taste, sprinkle with chopped parsley and serve.

Note: If you like spicy food, add 10 ml (2 tsp) ground cumin and 10 ml (2 tsp) chopped fresh coriander to the pan while frying the onion and garlic for this dish.

Date & Ginger Towers with Toffee Sauce
(page 190)

FAR NORTH LEEK, MUSHROOM & HORSERADISH PIE

FAR NORTH HOTEL
Durness, Highland
Nick & Mary Weatherhead
.

Leeks and mushrooms flavoured with horseradish, topped by a crisp pie crust. Serve with creamed spinach and jacket potatoes.

Serves 4

100 g (4 oz) butter
500 g (1 lb) leeks, washed and diced
500 g (1 lb) mushrooms, washed and sliced
30 ml (2 tbsp) horseradish sauce
15 ml (1 tbsp) lemon juice
seasoning
250–500 g (10–16 oz) shortcrust pastry
beaten egg to glaze

1. Preheat the oven to 220°C (425°F) mark 7.
2. In a large saucepan, melt half the butter and sauté the leeks and mushrooms for 6–8 minutes until the leeks are transparent. Add the horseradish and allow the mixture to simmer for a further minute.
3. Spoon the leek mixture into a large pie dish. Dot with the remaining butter, pour over lemon juice and seasoning, then allow to cool.
4. On a lightly floured surface, roll out the pastry and use to cover the pie. Decorate with pastry trimmings and brush with a little beaten egg to glaze.
5. Bake in the hot oven for 15 minutes, then reduce the oven temperature to 170°C (325°F) mark 3 and continue cooking for 15 minutes until the pastry is golden brown.

VEGETABLE DISHES & SALADS

MINTED POTATO CAKES

GREEN LAWNS HOTEL
Falmouth, Cornwall

Robert Collings with chef Patrick Quinn

.

Creamed potatoes flavoured with mint, shaped into small round patties and fried until crisp. An ideal potato dish to serve with lamb.

Serves 4

500 g (1 lb) potatoes, peeled
25 g (1 oz) butter, softened
1 egg yolk
10 ml (2 tsp) mint, chopped finely
seasoning
flour
50 g (2 oz) butter for frying
30 ml (2 tbsp) oil for frying

1.   In a pan of boiling, salted water, cook the potatoes until tender. Drain thoroughly, then mash or force through a sieve into a mixing bowl, to make a smooth purée. Stir in the softened butter, egg yolk, mint and seasoning.
2.   Divide the potato into 4 or 8 lumps and on a lightly floured work surface roll each into round, burger-like shapes. Arrange the potato cakes on a tray and refrigerate for at least 30 minutes to firm the mixture.
3.   Heat the butter and oil together in a frying pan and when the fat is piping hot, fry the cakes for 2–3 minutes on each side. Turn carefully with a fish slice, until both sides are crisp and golden brown. Drain thoroughly on kitchen paper before serving.

LEEK & POTATO FRITTERS

TREWITHEN RESTAURANT
Lostwithiel, Cornwall

Mr & Mrs B.F. Rolls

.

Fried leek and potato cakes, flavoured with nutmeg. Serve with grilled meats.

Serves 6

2 medium leeks, sliced very thinly
500 g (1 lb) potatoes, grated
3 eggs, lightly beaten
seasoning
grated nutmeg
oil or clarified butter for frying

1.   Blanch the sliced leeks in boiling, salted water for 2 minutes until softened. Drain thoroughly.
2.   In a bowl, mix together the leeks, grated potato, eggs, seasoning and nutmeg.
3.   Heat a little oil or clarified butter in a frying pan. When the oil is very hot, drop a sixth of the mixture into the fat, quickly spreading with a spatula to form a flat patty. Carefully turn and continue to fry until both sides are golden. Drain on kitchen paper and serve.

POTATO CASSEROLE

LONG'S RESTAURANT
Truro, Cornwall

Ian & Ann Long

.

Sliced potatoes, layered with onions and baked in stock. This is the ideal potato dish for entertaining as it has a reasonably elastic cooking time, looks impressive and complements most dishes. If serving these potatoes with a plain grilled meal, sprinkle a little grated cheese over the top towards the end of cooking, or use a half-and-half mix of milk and stock for the cooking liquid.

Serves 8

500 ml (1 pint) good beef stock (see page 200)
3 medium onions, thinly sliced
5 ml (1 tsp) butter
1.5 kg (3 lb) potatoes, peeled
seasoning
5 ml (1 tsp) dried thyme
butter or dripping to finish

1. Preheat the oven to 170°C (325°F) mark 3.
2. Heat the stock in a saucepan, add the onions and butter, cook for 1 minute, then strain and reserve both the onions and the stock.
3. Bring a large pan of salted water to the boil. Cut the potatoes into 3 mm (⅛ inch) thick slices and cook in the boiling water for 4 minutes. Strain and rinse the potatoes under cold water.
4. Layer the potatoes and onions in a flat ovenproof casserole dish, sprinkling with seasoning and thyme as you layer. Finish with a layer of potatoes. Pour in enough stock to come just below the top layer.
5. Bake in the hot oven for 1½ hours. Remove the dish from the oven and raise the temperature to 220°C (425°F) mark 7.
6. Using a potato masher or fork, press the potatoes gently down into the stock, to spread a little liquid over the top. Dot with butter or dripping and return the dish to the oven for 15 minutes until the top is brown and crispy.

LIME-SCENTED RICE

LE GRANDGOUSIER
Brighton, Sussex

Mr L.M. Harris with chef O.P. Godfrey

.

Rice, flavoured with lime zest and juice. Serve with fish and chicken.

Serves 4–6

200 g (8 oz) white long grain rice, rinsed
juice and grated zest of 2 limes
butter for greasing

1. Bring plenty of salted water to the boil in a large saucepan, add the rice, half the lime zest and the juice and boil rapidly for 12–15 minutes until the rice is just tender.
2. Drain and rinse, then stir through the remaining lime zest and juice. Arrange the rice in a lightly buttered serving dish or bowl. Cover and keep warm in a moderate oven until ready to serve.

PARSNIP & PEAR CASSEROLE GARNISHED WITH WALNUTS

LONG'S RESTAURANT
Truro, Cornwall

Ian & Ann Long

•

Parsnips and pears baked in cream, topped with a layer of crisp breadcrumbs. Serve with game or plain roast meats.

Serves 8

1 kg (2 lb) parsnips, peeled
juice of 1 lemon
500 g (1 lb) dessert pears
75 g (3 oz) butter, melted
seasoning
30 ml (2 tbsp) brown sugar
250 ml (10 fl oz) double cream
60–90 ml (4–6 tbsp) brown breadcrumbs

To serve:
15 g (½ oz) butter
24 walnut halves

1. Slice the parsnips into even rounds. Bring a pan of salted water to the boil, add the parsnips and cook for 2 minutes. Drain and refresh under cold running water.
2. Mix the lemon juice with a little water in a small bowl.
3. Peel the pears. Cut in half lengthwise, then use a teaspoon to remove the pips and tough thread that runs up the centre of the fruit. Slice across the pears to form even pieces, placing them in the lemon water as you cut (this should prevent them turning brown).
4. Brush some of the melted butter over a shallow ovenproof dish. Arrange the parsnip slices in a layer over the base of the dish. Sprinkle with seasoning and sugar. Pour over an even coating of cream. Cover with an overlapping layer of pears, season and add a coating of cream. Build up alternate layers, finishing with a layer of parsnips. Brush the top with the remaining melted butter and press the breadcrumbs onto the surface, to form an even topping. Refrigerate until required.
5. Preheat the oven to 170°C (325°F) mark 3.
6. Cook the parsnip casserole at the top of the hot oven for 45 minutes, raising the heat to 200°C (400°F) mark 6 for the last 5 minutes.
7. Prepare the garnish. Melt the butter and sauté the walnuts until they shine. Arrange around the dish and serve.

BRAISED CELERY HEARTS

LONG'S RESTAURANT
Truro, Cornwall

Ian & Ann Long

.

Celery hearts, braised in beef stock, topped with sliced Parma ham and grated lemon zest. Serve with casseroles or grilled food.

Serves 8

4 heads of celery
30 ml (2 tbsp) light olive oil
250 ml (10 fl oz) beef stock (see page 200)
seasoning
75 g (3 oz) Parma ham
butter for greasing
grated zest of 1 lemon

1.   Trim the celery to about 12.5 cm (5 inches) from the base, shave away any brown at the root end, leaving the sticks joined together at the base. Scrub the trimmed hearts clean. (Use the celery trimmings in soups and stocks.)
2.   Immerse the celery in boiling, salted water, cook for 10 minutes, then drain in a colander, rinse under cold running water and pat dry on a clean tea towel.
3.   Cut the celery hearts in half lengthwise.
4.   Heat the oil in a large frying pan. Put the celery pieces rounded side down in the hot oil and cook until browned. Using a spatula, carefully turn the celery to brown the other side.
5.   Pour the stock into the pan, season with salt and bring to the boil, lower the heat, cover and leave to simmer for 40 minutes until the celery is tender.
6.   Slice the Parma ham into thin strips.
7.   Using a slotted spoon, transfer the celery to a buttered, warm serving dish. If the braising liquid is still thin, return the pan to the heat and boil until reduced and thickened. Grate black pepper into the liquid to taste and ladle over the celery.
8.   Sprinkle the ham and grated lemon zest over the celery. Serve while piping hot.

SPICED WHITE CABBAGE

LONG'S RESTAURANT
Truro, Cornwall

Ian & Ann Long

•

A crisp and spicy cabbage stir-fry. Serve with plain grilled steaks.

Serves 8

1 medium Dutch white cabbage
30 ml (2 tbsp) light vegetable or hazelnut oil
1 onion, sliced
2 cloves garlic, crushed
5 ml (1 tsp) salt
2.5 ml (½ tsp) chilli powder
2.5 ml (½ tsp) coriander, ground
2.5 ml (½ tsp) cumin, ground
15 ml (1 tbsp) sultanas
15 ml (1 tbsp) desiccated coconut

1.   Remove and discard the outer leaves of the cabbage, cut into quarters and slice as thinly as possible.
2.   Heat the oil in a large frying pan or wok. Add the onion, garlic and spices, and toss for 1 minute.
3.   Add the cabbage and turn until the mixture is glossy. Add the sultanas and coconut, continue tossing for a few minutes and serve.

Note: Don't overcook this dish; the cabbage should still be crisp when it is served.

BROAD BEANS WITH MUSTARD SAUCE

LONG'S RESTAURANT
Truro, Cornwall

Ian & Ann Long

•

Broad beans in a creamy mustard sauce. Serve with roasts, nut loaf or plain grilled fish.

Serves 8

25 g (1 oz) butter
15 ml (1 tbsp) flour
500 ml (1 pint) milk
15 ml (1 tbsp) English mustard powder
15 ml (1 tbsp) red wine vinegar
5 ml (1 tsp) caster sugar
seasoning
500 g (1 lb) broad beans, shelled

1.   Melt the butter in a saucepan, stir in the flour to form a roux and cook for 2 minutes until sandy in texture. Gradually add the milk, reduce the heat and stir until thick. Remove from the heat.
2.   In a bowl, mix together the mustard, vinegar and sugar until smooth, then whisk into the white sauce. Taste and season.
3.   Cook the broad beans in boiling, salted water.
4.   Reheat the mustard sauce. Drain the beans, then return to the hot saucepan and toss for a few seconds until dry. Add the beans to the mustard sauce, pour into a warm dish and serve.

OLD HALL ONION RINGS

OLD HALL HOTEL
Buxton, Derbyshire

Mrs Louise Potter with chef Mr J.R. Lath

Crisp, fried batter-coated onion rings. Serve hot with grilled meats.

Serves 4–6

200 g (8 oz) flour
salt
1 egg, lightly beaten
125 ml (5 fl oz) milk
2 onions, sliced
oil for frying

1.   Sift the flour and a pinch of salt into a large bowl. Make a hollow in the centre and add the egg, followed by half the milk. Stir until all the flour is mixed in, then beat with an electric whisk until the batter is smooth.
2.   Add the remaining milk and whisk once more until the mixture is light and frothy. Leave to stand for 10 minutes.
3.   Separate the onion slices to form individual rings, dip the rings in the batter and carefully lower into hot oil. Deep fry until golden. Drain on kitchen paper and sprinkle with salt before serving.

WILD RICE & APRICOT SALAD

FOOD FOR THOUGHT
Covent Garden, London

Vanessa Garrett with chef Jane Stimpson

.

A salad of wild rice, apricots, watercress and marinated raw mushrooms. Serve as a light meal on its own, or with a slice of quiche and a small green salad.

Serves 4

For the mushroom marinade:
1 clove garlic, crushed
30 ml (2 tbsp) tamari (available from health food shops)
40 ml (8 tsp) vegetable stock
20 ml (4 tsp) tomato purée
2.5 ml (½ tsp) honey
10 ml (2 tsp) lemon juice
225 g (9 oz) mushrooms, sliced

For the salad:
100 g (4 oz) wild rice
125 g (5 oz) watercress, finely chopped
100 g (4 oz) dried apricots, finely chopped

1.   Combine all the marinade ingredients together in a large bowl, stir to mix thoroughly and coat all the mushrooms in liquid. Cover and leave for 1 hour.
2.   Cook the rice in boiling salted water for 25 minutes until soft and starting to split. Drain, rinse and leave to cool.
3.   Mix the rice, watercress and apricots into the mushroom bowl, stir to coat with marinade and serve.

ARAME & ALFALFA SALAD

FOOD FOR THOUGHT
Covent Garden, London

Vanessa Garrett with chef Jane Stimpson

.

A seaweed and alfalfa salad with sesame and orange dressing. Serve with any of the vegetarian main courses in this book.

Serves 4

For the salad:
15 g (½ oz) dried arame seaweed (available from health food shops)
15 ml (1 tbsp) tamari (available from health food shops)
50 g (2 oz) alfalfa sprouts
100 g (4 oz) smoked tofu, thinly sliced
½ red pepper, finely chopped
3 spring onions, finely chopped
25 g (1 oz) chopped parsley
1 orange, peeled and cut into segments

For the dressing:
10 ml (2 tsp) sesame oil
10 ml (2 tsp) rice vinegar
30 ml (2 tbsp) orange juice
10 ml (2 tsp) olive oil
5 ml (1 tsp) tamari (available from health food shops)
10 ml (2 tsp) caster sugar
5 ml (1 tsp) lemon juice
seasoning

1.   In a large bowl, cover the arame with hot water, stir in the tamari and leave for 5 minutes. Drain.
2.   Combine all the salad ingredients in a large bowl, stirring to ensure even distribution.
3.   Place all the dressing ingredients together in a screw-top jar and shake until thoroughly mixed. Pour over the salad and serve.

ENSALADILLA RUSSA

LA GIRALDA
Pinner, Middlesex

Mr D. Brown

.

Russian salad with prawns and tuna fish. Serve with cold meats or as part of a buffet spread.

Serves 8–10

500 g (1 lb) potatoes
150 g (6 oz) peas
150 g (6 oz) carrots, diced
200 g (8 oz) peeled prawns
200 g (8 oz) tuna fish
1 × 397 g (14 oz) can of red peppers, chopped
1 large onion, finely sliced
3 hard-boiled eggs, peeled and quartered
500 ml (1 pint) mayonnaise
seasoning

1.   Boil the potatoes in their skins until tender, then drain, cool, peel and slice.
2.   Cook the peas and carrots in boiling salted water until just tender. Drain and cool.
3.   Stir all the ingredients, except the eggs, into the mayonnaise. Mould into an attractive shape on a serving dish and decorate with the quartered eggs. Chill thoroughly before serving.

PICKLES & SAUCES

CHAKCHOUKA

MATAAM MARAKESH
Torquay, Devon

Mrs N. Birkett

.

A spicy pepper and tomato sauce. Serve hot with kebabs, barbecued chicken wings or sliced roast lamb, or cold with salads and chunks of cheese. Use a mixture of red, green, yellow and orange peppers to produce a colourful Chakchouka.

Serves 8

500 g (1 lb) peppers
500 g (1 lb) tomatoes, peeled and diced
25 g (1 oz) chopped parsley
25 g (1 oz) chopped coriander
2 cloves garlic, crushed
15 ml (1 tbsp) sweet paprika
1.25 ml (¼ tsp) chilli powder
1.25 ml (¼ tsp) cumin
1.25 ml (¼ tsp) salt
50 ml (2 fl oz) olive oil

1.   Grill the peppers until the skins char and burst, peel and dice.
2.   Place all the ingredients together in a large saucepan, stir and bring to the boil. Reduce the heat and simmer for 30–35 minutes until the sauce thickens and the flavours have blended.
Use as required.

Note: Small pots of this sauce will freeze successfully.

My Gran's Tomato & Apple Chutney

THE JEFFERSON ARMS
Thorganby, North Yorkshire

Robert Mason

·

A chunky tomato and apple chutney. Serve with cold meats or good Cheddar cheese.

For approximately 2.5 kg (5 lb) chutney

1 kg (2 lb) ripe tomatoes, skinned
1 kg (2 lb) apples
500 g (1 lb) onions, finely chopped
200 g (8 oz) sultanas
5 ml (1 tsp) dry mustard
5 ml (1 tsp) ground ginger
5 ml (1 tsp) salt
500 g (1 lb) brown sugar
750 ml (1½ pints) spiced or wine vinegar

1.   Cut the skinned tomatoes into thick slices and place in a large preserving pan or saucepan.
2.   Wash the apples, do not peel but core and cut into small pieces. Add to the pan, together with all the other ingredients.
3.   Bring to the boil over a gentle heat, stirring until the sugar is dissolved. Reduce the heat and cook for 2 hours, stirring occasionally, until reduced and thickened.
4.   Ladle into warm, clean jars and cover when cold. Keep in a cool dark cupboard for 2 months before using.

BEETROOT PICKLE

VERONICA'S
Hereford Road, London
Mark Stapley & Veronica Shaw

·

A Victorian pickle recipe, based on the writings of Mrs Beeton. Serve with cold meats and salads.

Serves 6–8

6 medium beetroot
1 litre (2 pints) malt vinegar
15 g (½ oz) black pepper
15 g (½ oz) allspice
either 1 small horseradish root, grated
or 15 ml (1 tbsp) creamed horseradish

1. Wash the beetroot carefully; do not tear the skins or they will bleed. Cut off the leaf stalks 2.5–5 cm (1–2 inches) above the beetroot but do not trim the actual root until cooked.
2. Boil in lightly salted water for 1½ hours or until tender, drain and when cool enough to handle slide off the skins. Cut into 1.25 cm (½ inch) slices and stack in a clean pickle jar(s).
3. While the beetroot is cooking, boil the vinegar, pepper, spice and horseradish together for 10 minutes, leave to cool completely, then pour over the beetroot.
4. Cover the jar(s) with vinegar-proof lids and store in a cool dry place until required.

FIVE HERB SAUCE

LE GRANDGOUSIER
Brighton, Sussex
Mr L.M. Harris with chef Mr. O.P. Godfrey

·

A fresh-tasting herby oil. Use to brush over fish or meat while grilling, or as the basis for barbecue marinades. Prepare in summer when fresh herbs are plentiful and store in a dark cupboard for use throughout the winter.

For 1 litre (2 pints)

50 g (2 oz) fresh sorrel
50 g (2 oz) fresh basil
50 g (2 oz) fresh tarragon
50 g (2 oz) fresh chervil
50 g (2 oz) fresh flat leaf parsley
500 ml (1 pint) olive oil

1. Finely chop all the herbs. Mix the herbs and olive oil together in a large jug.
2. Leave at room temperature for 1 hour, bottle, seal and store in a dark cupboard or use as required.

SORREL & BASIL SAUCE

LE GRANDGOUSIER
Brighton, Sussex

Mr L.M. Harris with chef Mr O.P. Godfrey

A sharp herb sauce that goes well with plain poached or grilled fish.

Serves 6

1 small onion, finely chopped
125 ml (5 fl oz) good fish stock (see page 200)
15 ml (1 tbsp) white wine vinegar
10 sorrel leaves
2 spinach leaves
25 g (1 oz) basil leaves
5 ml (1 tsp) soy sauce
25 g (1 oz) unsalted butter
25 ml (1 fl oz) double cream
40 ml (1½ fl oz) yogurt

1. In a small pan, heat together the onion, stock and vinegar. Bring to the boil and simmer until reduced to a quarter of the volume.
2. Place all the other ingredients together in the liquidiser, add the reduced liquid and onion. Process until completely smooth, then chill until required.

VICTORIAN ENGLISH SAUCE FOR SALADS

VERONICA'S
Hereford Road, London

Mark Stapley & Veronica Shaw

．

Sharp, light, creamy salad dressing, a cross between mayonnaise and salad cream. Serve with salads or use to accompany cold meats and fish. This recipe is taken from the 1845 cookery writings of Eliza Acton. The sauce will keep for 3 days in the refrigerator, but is best eaten when freshly prepared.

Serves 4–6

3 egg yolks, hard-boiled
2.5 ml (½ tsp) salt
5 ml (1 tsp) sugar
pinch of cayenne
20 ml (4 tsp) water
125 ml (5 fl oz) whipping cream
20 ml (4 tsp) white wine or tarragon vinegar
dash of Tabasco
2 cloves garlic, crushed

1. In a bowl, mash together the hard-boiled egg yolks, salt, sugar, cayenne and water.
2. Gradually add the cream, vinegar, Tabasco and garlic, a drop at a time, beating continuously, until the sauce thickens.
3. Refrigerate until required.

PUDDINGS & DESSERTS

ROSE PETAL ICE CREAM

AYTON HALL HOTEL
Low Green, North Yorkshire

Melvin Rhodes

.

A soft ice cream, flavoured with rosewater. Serve scooped into cup-shaped tulip biscuits, or set in a bombe mould and surrounded by washed fresh rose buds. Prepare this recipe when you have several hours to spare, as it is important to whisk the mixture frequently during the freezing process.

Serves 4–6

5 egg yolks
200 g (8 oz) caster sugar
finely grated zest and juice of 1 lemon
250 ml (10 fl oz) milk
1 vanilla pod or 2.5 ml (½ tsp) vanilla essence
100 g (4 oz) lemon curd
250 ml (10 fl oz) double cream
10–15 ml (2–3 tsp) rosewater
5 ml (1 tsp) concentrated raspberry juice or red food
colouring to taste (optional)

To serve:
wafer biscuits

1. In a mixing bowl, beat together the egg yolks and sugar until pale and creamy. Add the lemon zest and juice.
2. Bring the milk and vanilla to the boil in a saucepan, then whisk into the egg yolk mixture. Pour the resulting liquid into a clean saucepan and return to the heat. Whisk in the lemon curd and continue to heat until the liquid is frothing vigorously around the edges, 74°C (175°F) on the thermometer.

3. Remove the pan from the heat and whisk the liquid into the cream. Cover and leave at room temperature to cool as quickly as possible. Add the rosewater and colouring to taste, but remember the flavour grows stronger during freezing.

4. When cool, pour the liquid into a freezer container, cover and freeze for 2 hours, until a thick rim has formed around the edge.

5. Remove from the freezer, beat with an electric whisk, then return to the freezer. Continue beating every hour until the ice cream is too hard to whisk, approximately 6 times. The more you whisk, the smaller the ice crystals will be and the smoother the texture of the resulting ice cream.

6. Remove the ice cream from the freezer 10 minutes before serving to soften and let the flavour develop.

CRANACHAN

HOTEL EILEAN IARMAIN
Isle of Skye

Mr Iain Noble

.

A thick-set cream, flavoured with honey and whisky, topped with crisp oatmeal and soft fruit.

Serves 6

40 g (1½ oz) pinhead oatmeal
500 ml (1 pint) double cream
45 ml (3 tbsp) clear heather honey
50 g (2 oz) Crowdie, Scottish soft cheese, or yogurt
45 ml (3 tbsp) whisky
125 g (5 oz) soft fruit (a mixture of raspberries and blackcurrants is recommended)

To serve:
shortbread fingers

1. Toast the oatmeal under a hot grill until it is crisp and golden. Leave to cool.

2. Whip the cream until it forms soft peaks. Stir in the honey, Crowdie or yogurt and whisky.

3. Spoon the mixture into 6 individual glasses or 1 large serving dish and chill thoroughly.

4. Sprinkle the oatmeal evenly over the top of the cream and arrange the soft fruit in the centre.

5. Serve chilled with shortbread fingers.

GLAYVA CRUNCH

CRINGLETIE HOUSE HOTEL
Peebles, Borders
Stanley & Aileen Maguire

.

A light whisky and vanilla flavoured cream, layered with oatmeal, nuts and grated chocolate.

Serves 4–6

100 g (4 oz) oatmeal, toasted
100 g (4 oz) almonds, chopped and toasted
100 g (4 oz) chocolate, grated
500 ml (1 pint) double cream
25 g (1 oz) caster sugar
45 ml (3 tbsp) Glayva whisky
1.25 ml (¼ tsp) vanilla essence
2 egg whites

1.   In a bowl, mix together the oatmeal, nuts and chocolate.
2.   In a separate bowl, whip together the cream, sugar, whisky and vanilla until it holds its shape but is not too stiff.
3.   Separately whisk the egg whites until stiff, then gently fold into the cream.
4.   Layer the cream and oatmeal mixtures in wine glasses, starting with the cream mixture and finishing with a layer of oatmeal on top. Chill thoroughly before serving.

ICED CHOCOLATE TERRINE

LE RENOIR
Charing Cross Road, London
Robbie Helbawi with chef Didier Neveu

.

A frozen layered terrine of white and dark chocolate, served with a rich custard sauce.

Serves 8–10

50 g (2 oz) unsalted butter
75 g (3 oz) plain chocolate
75 g (3 oz) white chocolate
5 eggs, separated
25 g (1 oz) caster sugar
30 ml (2 tbsp) Kahlua
50 ml (2 fl oz) double cream

To serve:
crème Anglaise (see page 205)

1. Remember this is a layered terrine of 2 chocolate mixtures, so every part of the method is duplicated, once for the white chocolate, once for the dark.
2. Divide the butter between 2 bowls. Add the dark chocolate to 1 bowl, the white chocolate to the other. Place the bowls over pans of hot water and heat to melt both the chocolate and butter. Remove the bowls from the heat.
3. While the chocolate is melting, whisk the egg yolks and sugar together in a bowl until pale and creamy, then add the Kahlua.
4. In another bowl, whip the cream until it forms soft peaks.
5. In a third bowl, whip the egg whites until stiff.
6. Fold half the egg yolk mixture into each chocolate mix, half of the cream into each, followed by half of the stiff egg white.
7. Pour the dark chocolate mix into the base of a long, thin loaf or terrine mould and place in the freezer for 1½ hours until set. Leave the white chocolate mixture, covered, at room temperature while the dark chocolate is setting.
8. As soon as the dark chocolate has set, pour the white chocolate mixture on top and return the terrine to the freezer for at least 4 hours.
9. Remove the terrine from the freezer 2 minutes before it is required, turn out of the mould and slice thinly. Serve individual slices on dessert plates, surrounded with crème Anglaise.

Note: To loosen the terrine from the mould, run a knife around the edge, then dip the base into hot water and count to 5. Remove from the water and dry the outside of the mould. Turn the mould over on a serving plate or cutting board and shake plate and mould together until the terrine moves!

CHOCOLATE MOUSSE WITH COINTREAU

DOWN'S OF MAYFAIR
Mayfair, London

Chris Kerridge

.

A rich chocolate mousse laced with Cointreau and topped with cream.

Serves 6–8

8 eggs, separated
125 g (5 oz) cooking chocolate
125 g (5 oz) good dessert chocolate
40 ml (1½ fl oz) Cointreau

To serve:
whipped cream
chocolate curls or grated orange zest

1. In a bowl, beat the egg whites until stiff.
2. In a double boiler or bowl set over a saucepan of hot water, heat the chocolate until it melts, then remove from the heat.
3. In a bowl, mix the egg yolks and Cointreau together and add to the melted chocolate. Gently fold in the egg whites.
4. Spoon the mixture into individual ramekins or wine glasses and chill for at least 30 minutes. Decorate with rosettes of cream and chocolate curls or grated orange zest before serving.

RASPBERRY CHOCOLATE BOX

THE CROWN OF CRUCIS
Ampney Crucis, Gloucestershire

Mr R.K. Mills

.

A rich chocolate and raspberry fridge cake gâteau. For ultimate decadence, serve with a sauce of fresh puréed raspberries, sweetened with icing sugar and flavoured with brandy.

Serves 8

75 g (3 oz) butter
100 g (4 oz) good quality cooking chocolate
500 g (1 lb) chocolate sponge cake
50 g (2 oz) raisins
45 ml (3 tbsp) brandy
250 ml (10 fl oz) double cream
200 g (8 oz) raspberries (use frozen fruit if fresh is not available)
10 ml (2 tsp) caster sugar (optional)
15–20 thin chocolate mint crisps (NOT cream-filled ones)

1.   Melt the butter and chocolate together in a double boiler or pan set over a bowl of hot water.
2.   Crumble the chocolate sponge into a mixing bowl, pour on the melted chocolate and mix thoroughly until it resembles a thick, uncooked cake mixture.
3.   Add the raisins and brandy.
4.   Mould half the cake mixture into an oblong, approximately 20 × 10 × 1.25 cm (8 × 4 × ½ inch) on a serving plate. The mixture will require encouragement from clean fingers and a palette knife to form the oblong!
5.   Whip the cream until it forms soft peaks, then use a third of it to cover the top of your chocolate layer.
6.   Cover the cream with half the raspberries and sprinkle with sugar.
7.   On a sheet of greaseproof paper, form the rest of the sponge into an oblong the same size as the first. Chill until set, then carefully place on top of the raspberry layer by turning it upside down over the cake and peeling away the greaseproof paper.
8.   Spread or pipe a third of the cream over the top of the cake, and decorate with the remaining raspberries.
9.   Coat the sides of the cake with the remaining cream, then press the chocolate mints into the edges. Refrigerate until required.

Note: It makes serving a lot simpler if you position the mint crisps where they measure out the individual portions of this cake, with a slight gap between each mint for easy cutting.

CHOCOLATE & SPONGE FINGER PAVÉ

THE JEFFERSON ARMS
Thorganby, North Yorkshire

Robert Mason

·

Rum-soaked sponge fingers, layered with a rich chocolate cream.

Serves 6–8

50 g (2 oz) caster sugar
60 ml (4 tbsp) rum (white or dark)
100 g (4 oz) plain chocolate
50 g (2 oz) butter
100 g (4 oz) icing sugar
3 egg yolks
18 sponge fingers

To serve:
whipped double cream or chocolate butter cream

1.   In a small saucepan, melt half the sugar with 60 ml (4 tbsp) water and bring to the boil. Remove from the heat and stir in the rum.
2.   Melt the chocolate in a double boiler or bowl set over a pan of hot water.
3.   In a mixing bowl, beat together the butter and icing sugar until light and fluffy, then beat in the egg yolks. Stir in the melted chocolate.
4.   Dip several sponge fingers into the rum syrup, leave for several seconds to absorb some of the liquid but not too long or they will dissolve. Layer the fingers over the base of a loose-bottomed, long, thin cake tin or separating loaf tin. Spread with a layer of chocolate, followed by another layer of sponge fingers. Continue to layer until the tin is full or there is no more mixture.
5.   Refrigerate for 2 hours until the chocolate is set.
6.   Turn the pavé out onto a serving plate, pipe the top with whipped cream or butter cream and serve.

CHOCOLATE ALPINI

BRADFORD ARMS & RESTAURANT
Llanymynech, Shropshire

Michael & Anne Murphy

·

Fingers of whisky-flavoured chocolate biscuit cake served with cream.

Serves 8–10

500 g (1 lb) butter
500 g (1 lb) plain chocolate
50–75 ml (2–3 fl oz) whisky
125 ml (5 fl oz) single or whipping cream
300 g (12 oz) digestive biscuits, crushed
200 g (8 oz) mixed nuts, chopped

To serve:
whipped cream

1.   Melt the butter and chocolate together in a double boiler or bowl set over a pan of hot water.
2.   Stir in the whisky and cream, then add the biscuit crumbs and nuts, mixing carefully to ensure all the nuts and crumbs are evenly coated in chocolate cream.
3.   Line a baking tray or cake tin with clingfilm so that a little film protrudes at each side. Alternatively, use a loose-bottomed cake tin to prepare the Alpini, which will not require lining. Spoon the mixture into the tin and spread flat. Refrigerate for 1 hour until the mixture has set.
4.   Remove the cake from the tin. If using a tin lined with clingfilm, gently pull at the visible plastic edges, then peel the film away from the base of the turned-out cake. Slice the cake very thinly and serve 2 or 3 slices per portion with a mound of whipped cream.

VACHERIN AU KIRSCH

RUDLOE PARK HOTEL
Corsham, Wiltshire
Mr I.C. Overend with chef Geoff Bell

·

Meringue ovals sandwiched with a kirsch-flavoured creamy mousse.

Serves 8–10

For the meringue:
6 egg whites
150 g (6 oz) granulated sugar
150 g (6 oz) caster sugar

For the filling:
15 g (½ oz) powdered gelatine
60 ml (4 tbsp) warm water
4 egg yolks
60 ml (4 tbsp) soft light brown sugar
60 ml (4 tbsp) kirsch
300 ml (12 fl oz) double cream

To serve:
icing sugar for dusting

1. Preheat the oven to 150°C (300°F) mark 2. Draw 2 ovals 15 cm × 30 cm (12 inches × 6 inches) on silicone paper and use to line 2 baking sheets, positioning the drawn line next to the metal.
2. In a large mixing bowl, beat together the egg whites and granulated sugar for 5–7 minutes until they form soft peaks. Fold in the caster sugar.
3. Divide the meringue in half and pile equal quantities onto each baking sheet. Use a spatula to spread the meringue into a level oval. Bake in the oven for 2 hours, until crisp. Turn off the oven but leave the meringues inside until cold. Remove from the baking paper.
4. Prepare the filling. Sprinkle the gelatine over the warm water and stir until completely dissolved.
5. Beat the egg yolks and sugar together, in a bowl, until white and fluffy, then add the kirsch.
6. Beat the cream until it forms soft peaks and fold into the egg mixture, then fold in the gelatine. Leave the filling mixture at room temperature for 15 minutes to thicken slightly.
7. Pipe or spread the filling over one of the meringue ovals and place the second meringue on top. Chill for 30 minutes until the filling has set. Dust the top of the vacherin with icing sugar and serve.

Pavlova

WYNDHAM ARMS
Clearwell, Gloucestershire

John Stanford with chef Paul Cooke

A large meringue nest filled with cream and seasonal fresh fruit. For the best results, use fruits that complement each other in colour and texture. For example, strawberries, raspberries and redcurrants or slices of kiwi fruit with seedless black and green grapes.

Serves 6–8

3 egg whites
150 g (6 oz) caster sugar
2.5 ml (½ tsp) vanilla essence
5 ml (1 tsp) cornflour
5 ml (1 tsp) white wine vinegar

For the topping:
250 ml (10 fl oz) double cream
seasonal fruits (as available)

1. Preheat the oven to 170°C (325°F) mark 3.
2. Draw a 20 cm (8 inch) diameter circle on silicone paper and use to line a baking sheet, positioning the drawn line next to the metal.
3. Whisk the egg whites until stiff, then gradually beat in the sugar, vanilla essence, cornflour and vinegar.
4. Pipe or spoon the meringue onto the silicone paper, using the line as a guide to form a circle. Pile slightly more mixture at the edges of the circle so the meringue forms a nest.
5. Bake in the preheated oven for 50–60 minutes, then turn off the heat and leave the meringue in the warm oven until completely cool.
6. Remove the meringue from the paper and place on a serving dish.
7. Whip the cream until stiff, pile into the meringue, top with plenty of fresh fruit and serve.

ICED DRAMBUIE MOUSSES

THE STEPPES
Ullingswick, Herefordshire
Henry & Tricia Howland

.

Creamy Drambuie-flavoured iced mousses that make a refreshing and luxurious end to a meal.

Serves 6

2 eggs, separated
300 ml (12 fl oz) double cream
60 ml (4 tbsp) Drambuie
100 g (4 oz) icing sugar

1. Whisk the egg whites until firm.
2. In a separate bowl, whisk the double cream, Drambuie, icing sugar and egg yolks together until firm.
3. Gently fold the egg whites into the cream, then pipe or spoon the mixture into 6 individual glasses or dishes.
4. Cover and freeze for at least 4 hours before serving.

GINGER CREAMS

LE GRANDGOUSIER
Brighton, Sussex
Mr L.M. Harris with chef Mr O.P. Godfrey

.

Individual ginger creams, flavoured with brandy and advocaat.

Serves 4

175 g (7 oz) ginger conserve
25 ml (1 fl oz) brandy
25 ml (1 fl oz) advocaat
300 ml (12 fl oz) double cream

To serve:
brandy snaps

1.   Put the ginger, brandy and advocaat into a bowl and whisk until creamy. Gradually whisk in the cream and beat until stiff.
2.   Spoon the mixture into individual ramekins or glasses and chill until required. Serve with brandy snap biscuits.

HOURGLASS CREAMS

HENLEY HOTEL
Bigbury-on-Sea, Devon

Mrs L. Beer

.

Treacle-flavoured milk jelly, set in individual glasses topped with clotted cream and grated chocolate. This traditional West Country recipe was originally created to use up the milk left after clotted cream manufacture.

Serves 4

15 g (½ oz) gelatine
60 ml (4 tbsp) water
500 ml (1 pint) milk
25 g (1 oz) vanilla sugar
15 ml (1 tbsp) black treacle
200 g (8 oz) clotted cream or whipped double cream
chocolate for grating

1.   Dissolve the gelatine in the water, gently warming the mixture in a small bowl set over a pan of water, until no gelatine granules are visible. Be careful not to overheat the gelatine or it will break down and the jelly will not set.
2.   In a saucepan, gently warm the milk, sugar and treacle to blood heat. Remove the pan from the heat and add the gelatine. Pour the mixture into individual wine glasses or serving bowls and refrigerate until set.
3.   Spread an even layer of clotted cream over the top of each jelly, sprinkle with grated chocolate and chill until required.

WHIM WHAM

VERONICA'S
Hereford Road, London

Mark Stapley & Veronica Shaw

·

A traditional 19th century recipe for an unusual layered sherry trifle.

Serves 6

500 ml (1 pint) double cream
125 ml (5 fl oz) sherry
grated zest of 1 lemon
50 g (2 oz) caster sugar
12 savoy biscuits (see page 204)
either 200 g (8 oz) redcurrant jelly
or 2 large fresh oranges, peeled and sliced
25 g (1 oz) candied peel, chopped

1. Whisk the cream, sherry, lemon zest and sugar together until thick.
2. Cut the biscuits into small pieces and use half of them to cover the base of a glass serving dish. Spread a third of the cream over the biscuits, then dot with little heaps of half the redcurrant jelly or orange slices. Fill the bowl by repeating the layers; biscuits, cream, jelly or oranges. Finish with a layer of cream.
3. Sprinkle the chopped peel over the top of the trifle and chill until ready to serve.

HAZELNUT MERINGUE CAKE WITH MELBA SAUCE

FLACKLEY ASH HOTEL
Peasmarsh, East Sussex

Clive & Jeanie Bennett

·

Hazelnut meringue circles, sandwiched together with cream and raspberries, served with a sharp raspberry sauce.

Serves 6–8

For the cake:
125 g (5 oz) hazelnuts
butter for greasing
5 egg whites
250 g (10 oz) caster sugar
3–4 drops vanilla essence
2.5 ml (½ tsp) vinegar

For the topping:
300 ml (12 fl oz) double cream
225 g (9 oz) raspberries (fresh or frozen)
15 ml (1 tbsp) icing sugar

For the sauce:
225 g (9 oz) raspberries
60 ml (4 tbsp) icing sugar, sifted

1.   If the hazelnuts have dark brown skins, place on a baking tray in a hot oven for 10 minutes, then rub vigorously between 2 layers of clean tea towel. This will remove the skins. Grind nuts into a fine paste in a coffee grinder or food processor.
2.   Lightly grease 2 × 20 cm (8 inch) sandwich tins and line with silicone paper. Preheat the oven to 190°C (375°F) mark 5.
3.   Whisk the egg whites until just stiff. Add the sugar, a little at a time, and continue beating until the mixture is stiff, shiny and all the sugar is incorporated.
4.   Gently fold the vanilla essence, vinegar and hazelnuts into the egg whites.
5.   Divide the meringue mixture between the tins, smoothing level with a palette knife. Bake in the preheated oven for 35–40 minutes until the top is crisp and the inside soft, but cooked. Turn off the oven, but leave the meringues inside to cool completely. Remove from the tins and peel off the silicone paper.
6.   Whisk the cream until stiff and pipe two thirds over the base meringue. Pile the raspberries over the cream, saving a few for the top. Decorate the second meringue circle with the remaining cream and raspberries, dust with icing sugar, then use to cover the base meringue. Chill until required.
7.   Prepare the Melba sauce. Purée the raspberries in a food processor then sieve, or rub the whole fruit through a nylon strainer. Gradually stir in the sifted icing sugar to taste and serve in a jug with slices of the meringue cake.

ORANGES WITH PRALINE CREAM

TREWITHEN RESTAURANT
Lostwithiel, Cornwall

Mr & Mrs B.F. Rolls

Orange segments, soaked in Grand Marnier, served with a rich praline cream and brandy snaps.

Serves 8

For the pastry cream:
250 ml (10 fl oz) milk
25 g (1 oz) caster sugar
15 g (½ oz) flour
15 ml (1 tbsp) cornflour
1 egg, lightly beaten
15 g (½ oz) butter

For the praline cream:
250 ml (10 fl oz) double cream
100 g (4 oz) praline (see page 204)
3–4 oranges
8 brandy snaps
45 ml (3 tbsp) Grand Marnier

1. First prepare the pastry cream. Warm the milk in a pan over a low heat. In a bowl, blend together the sugar, flour, cornflour and beaten egg. Gradually stir in the warmed milk. Return the mixture to the pan and stir continuously with a balloon whisk until the custard thickens and just comes to the boil. Remove from the heat and stir in the butter. Cover with greaseproof paper (to prevent a skin forming) and cool.
2. Whip the cream until stiff. Fold into the cool pastry cream and stir in the praline. Refrigerate until cold.
3. Cut several long thin strips of orange peel from the skin of the oranges, place in a pan with 125 ml (5 fl oz) water and bring to the boil to remove any bitterness and soften the strands. Drain.
4. Peel and segment the oranges. Arrange the segments in the shape of a fan to one side of individual serving plates. Place a spoonful of cream at the base of the fan and top with a brandy snap and a few orange peel strips. Drizzle the Grand Marnier over the orange segments and refrigerate until required.

ICED BISCUIT GLACÉ

LE GRANDGOUSIER
Brighton, Sussex

Mr L.M. Harris with chef Mr O.P. Godfrey

.

Individual honey and praline flavoured iced mousses. Try adding diced dried apricots, figs or prunes in place of the glacé cherries.

Serves 4–6

100 g (4 oz) sugar
100 ml (4 fl oz) water
50 g (2 oz) clear honey
175 ml (7 fl oz) double cream
2 eggs, separated
75 g (3 oz) glacé cherries, finely chopped
75 g (3 oz) mixed peel, finely chopped
75 g (3 oz) praline (see page 204)

To serve:
shortbread or wafer biscuits

1. Heat the sugar and water together until the sugar melts and white bubbles form across the top of the syrup. Stir in the honey, then leave to cool slightly.
2. Whip the cream until stiff.
3. In a bowl, gradually whisk half the cooled sugar syrup into the egg yolks.
4. In a separate bowl, whisk the egg whites until stiff, then carefully fold into the remaining sugar and honey mixture.
5. Fold the egg whites into the egg yolks, then fold in the cherries, mixed peel, praline and whipped cream, being careful not to over-fold the mixture or the air will be lost from the mousse and the fruit will sink.
6. Spoon the mixture into freezerproof glasses and freeze for at least 4 hours. Remove from the freezer for 5 minutes before serving with plain, sweet biscuits.

ETON MESS

VERONICA'S
Hereford Road, London

Mark Stapley & Veronica Shaw

.

Cream, laced with whisky-soaked strawberries, mixed with crushed meringues.

Serves 6

500 g (1 lb) strawberries
75 ml (3 fl oz) whisky
grated zest of 1 orange
375 ml (15 fl oz) double cream
6 meringues, crushed

1. Reserve a few strawberries for garnish and chop the remainder into a mixing bowl. Sprinkle with whisky and grated orange zest, cover and chill for 2–3 hours.
2. Whip the cream until it stands in soft peaks. Gently fold into the strawberries together with the crushed meringues.
3. Spoon the mixture into a glass serving dish, dot the top with the reserved strawberries and serve.

SUMMER PROFITEROLES

NETHERWOOD HOTEL
Grange-over-Sands, Cumbria

Messrs J.D. & M.P. Fallowfield

.

Large choux buns filled with cream and strawberries, topped by a rich chocolate sauce. When strawberries are out of season substitute with other fruit, such as kiwi fruit, black grapes, stoned black cherries or raspberries.

Serves 8

For the choux buns:
butter for greasing
50 g (2 oz) butter
125 ml (5 fl oz) water
65 g (2½ oz) strong plain flour
pinch of salt
2 eggs, lightly beaten
300 ml (12 fl oz) double cream, whipped
200 g (8 oz) strawberries, hulled and sliced

For the chocolate sauce:
200 g (8 oz) caster sugar
250 ml (10 fl oz) water
100 g (4 oz) cocoa powder

1. First prepare the choux buns. Preheat the oven to 220°C (425°F) mark 7 and lightly grease a baking sheet.
2. In a pan, heat together the butter and water until the butter has melted. Raise the temperature and bring the mixture to the boil.
3. Take the pan off the heat and quickly stir in the sifted flour and salt.
4. Return the pan to the heat and cook, stirring continuously, until the mixture leaves the sides of the pan clean and forms a ball in the centre.
5. Allow the mixture to cool to blood heat before adding the eggs, a little at a time, beating thoroughly after each addition.
6. Using a piping bag and wide nozzle, pipe 8 equal rounds of dough onto the baking sheet.
7. Bake in the hot oven for 15–20 minutes until golden, then cut a hole in the side of each choux bun (to allow steam to escape) and return the tray to the oven for a further 10 minutes.
8. Transfer the cooked buns to a wire rack and allow to cool.
9. Prepare the chocolate sauce. Place the sugar and water in a pan together. Stir over a low heat until the sugar dissolves, then bring the liquid to the boil and allow to simmer for 1 minute.
10. Whisk the cocoa powder into the sugar liquid until the sauce is smooth. Bring to the boil, then turn off the heat and leave to thicken and cool.
11. Cut the choux buns in half and fill the base with the whipped cream and strawberries.
12. Dip the bun top in chocolate sauce, then set over the strawberries and cream.
13. Serve chilled, with a jug of extra chocolate sauce for use by greedier guests!

STRAWBERRY SYLLABUB

LE GRANDGOUSIER
Brighton, Sussex

Mr L.M. Harris with chef Mr O.P. Godfrey

.

Individual strawberry creams served with plain, sweet biscuits.

Serves 4

500 g (1 lb) fresh strawberries
10 ml (2 tsp) lemon juice
375 ml (15 fl oz) double cream
8 egg whites
200 g (8 oz) sugar

To serve:
almond or shortbread biscuits

1. Liquidise the strawberries until smooth, then add the lemon juice.
2. In a bowl, whip the double cream until stiff.
3. In a separate bowl, whip the egg whites until stiff, then gradually whip in the sugar.
4. Gently fold the cream into the egg whites, followed by the strawberry purée.
5. Ladle the syllabub into individual serving dishes or glasses and refrigerate until set. Serve with almond or shortbread biscuits.

STRAWBERRY TOFFEE FLAN

THE KITCHEN
Polperro, Cornwall

Ian & Vanessa Bateson

.

Layers of crushed biscuits, toffee and strawberries topped with Cointreau-laced cream. Serve as suggested here, in one large cake, or prepare in individual glass dishes to show off the different layers.

Serves 8

1 × 405 g (14.3 oz) can condensed milk
50 g (2 oz) butter
100 g (4 oz) digestive biscuits, crushed
200 g (8 oz) strawberries
250 ml (10 fl oz) double cream
10 ml (2 tsp) caster sugar
100 ml (4 fl oz) Cointreau or Amaretto

1. In a heavy-based saucepan, cover the unopened can of condensed milk with water and bring to the boil. Simmer for 3 hours, topping up the water level regularly (the can will explode if the pan is allowed to boil dry). Leave to cool slightly.
2. Melt the butter and mix in the biscuit crumbs. Use to line a 20 cm (8 inch) loose-bottomed round cake tin or glass trifle bowl. Place in the fridge for an hour to set.
3. Open the can of condensed milk; it will now have a thick, toffee-like consistency. Spread over the biscuit base.
4. Slice the strawberries over the toffee, keeping a few back for decoration.
5. Whip the cream until stiff, whisk in the sugar, then add the Cointreau and continue beating until thick. Pipe or spoon the cream over the strawberries. Decorate with the reserved fruit and chill until ready to serve.
6. If using a loose-bottomed tin, remove the sides of the tin very carefully, leaving the base under the cake while serving.

LEMON & SHORTBREAD SANDWICHES ON HAZELNUT SAUCE

GREIG'S RESTAURANT
Barnes, London

Malcolm Greig with chef Malcolm Douglas

·

Individual circular shortbread biscuits sandwiched with brandy-laced, lemon soufflé, set on a creamy hazelnut sauce. If preparing the hazelnut sauce several hours in advance it will be necessary to add extra milk or single cream to ensure it has a runny consistency. Alternatively, warm the sauce gently before using to flood the plates.

Serves 8

For the shortbread:
125 g (5 oz) unsalted butter
65 g (2½ oz) caster sugar
125 g (5 oz) plain flour, sifted
65 g (2½ oz) ground rice
25 g (1 oz) vanilla sugar

For the lemon soufflé:
4 eggs, separated
50 g (2 oz) caster sugar
15 g (½ oz) gelatine
30 ml (2 tbsp) brandy
juice and finely grated zest of 4 lemons
250 ml (10 fl oz) whipping or double cream

For the sauce:
375 ml (15 fl oz) milk
50 g (2 oz) hazelnuts, ground
3 egg yolks
25 g (1 oz) caster sugar

To serve:
fresh mint leaves or pared lemon rind

1. For the shortbread, cream together the butter and sugar until soft and light. Gradually stir in the flour and rice until the mixture forms a smooth, soft dough. Divide the dough into 16 pieces. Select a pastry cutter that is slightly larger in diameter than your ramekins and position it on a baking sheet. Place each piece of dough in turn inside the pastry cutter and press out to make 16 circles. Chill.
2. Preheat the oven to 190°C (375°F) mark 5. Bake the shortbread circles in the preheated oven for 8–10 minutes until cooked but not browned, transfer to a wire rack and sprinkle with vanilla sugar. Cool.
3. Prepare the lemon soufflés. In a bowl, whisk the egg yolks and sugar together until thick and white.
4. While beating the egg yolks, soak the gelatine in the brandy until completely dissolved, gently heating if necessary. Whisk into the egg yolks and sugar, together with the lemon juice and zest.
5. In separate bowls, whip the cream and egg whites until stiff. Fold first the cream then the egg whites into the egg yolk mixture. Ladle the mixture into individual ramekins and leave to set.
6. Prepare the sauce. In a pan, heat together the milk and half the ground hazelnuts until almost boiling. Mix together the egg yolks and sugar in a bowl and pour the hot milk onto the eggs, stirring as you pour. Return the mixture to the pan and heat gently, stirring constantly until the mixture thickens to a coating consistency. Strain the sauce while still warm and stir in the remaining hazelnuts.

7. Flood a dinner plate with sauce and place a shortbread circle in the middle. Run a knife around the edge of the lemon soufflé and turn out onto the shortbread. (It may help to dip the base of the ramekin into warm water for a few seconds before up-turning.) Top with another shortbread circle to form the sandwich, garnish with mint leaves, strands of lemon rind or fresh fruit and serve.

CORNISH CHEESECAKE

TYGWYN GUEST HOUSE
Newquay, Cornwall

Mel, Clive & Mark Griffin

.

A creamy lemon cheesecake, set on a crushed biscuit base, topped with a layer of black cherries in kirsch-flavoured syrup.

Serves 6–8

65 g (2½ oz) butter
150 g (6 oz) digestive biscuits, crushed
300 g (12 oz) full fat soft cheese or curd cheese
30 ml (2 tbsp) lemon juice
30 ml (2 tbsp) caster sugar
150 g (6 oz) clotted cream
1 × 397 g (14 oz) can stoned black cherries
10 ml (2 tsp) arrowroot
30 ml (2 tbsp) icing sugar
15 ml (1 tbsp) kirsch (or extra to taste)

1. Melt the butter and mix into the biscuit crumbs. Press into the base of a 20 cm (8 inch) loose-bottomed cake tin and chill until firm.
2. In a mixing bowl, cream the soft cheese by working with the back of a wooden spoon, add the lemon juice and sugar, stirring until smooth, then add the clotted cream. Spoon this mixture over the biscuit base, spread level and chill until set.
3. Drain the tin of cherries, saving 125 ml (5 fl oz) of the juice. Arrange a layer of cherries over the top of the cake.
4. In a small bowl, mix the arrowroot, icing sugar and kirsch together to form a smooth paste. Bring the reserved cherry juice to the boil in a saucepan, pour onto the arrowroot paste and return the mixture to the heat, stirring constantly until the liquid has cleared and thickened. Leave to cool slightly.
5. Spoon the sauce over the cherries, to form an even, shiny, jelly-like layer. Refrigerate for at least 1 hour before serving.

PINA VELAZQUEZ

LA GIRALDA
Pinner, Middlesex

Mr D. Brown
.

Sliced fresh pineapple rings, coated in a sugar glaze, set on slices of brioche, soaked in rum and spread with pastry cream.

Serves 6

For the pastry cream:
125 ml (5 fl oz) milk
15 g (½ oz) caster sugar
7.5 g (¼ oz) flour
5 ml (1 tsp) cornflour
1 egg, lightly beaten
7.5 g (¼ oz) butter

For the cake:
200 g (8 oz) sugar
500 ml (1 pint) water
6 thick slices fresh pineapple, cored
1 small loaf of brioche
45 ml (3 tbsp) dark rum
30 ml (2 tbsp) apricot jam

1. First prepare the pastry cream. Warm the milk in a pan over a low heat. In a bowl, blend together the sugar, flour, cornflour and beaten egg. Gradually stir in the warmed milk. Return the mixture to the pan and stir continuously with a balloon whisk until the custard thickens and just comes to the boil. Remove from the heat and stir in the butter. Cover with greaseproof paper (to prevent a skin forming) and leave to cool completely.

2. Now, prepare the cake. Heat together the sugar and water until the sugar is dissolved. Place the pineapple in the syrup and poach over a gentle heat for 10 minutes. Remove the pineapple from the syrup and leave to cool and drain on wire racks.

3. Slice the brioche to form 6 × 2.5 cm (1 inch) thick slices. Sprinkle with the rum.

4. Spread each brioche slice with pastry cream and position a pineapple ring on top.

5. Heat the apricot jam with 10 ml (2 tsp) water until runny, sieve to remove any fruit pieces and brush the resulting clear glaze over the pineapple with a pastry brush.

6. Arrange on a serving dish and chill until required.

Passion Fruit Sorbet Trewithen Style

TREWITHEN RESTAURANT
Lostwithiel, Cornwall

Mr & Mrs B.F. Rolls

·

Home-made passion fruit granita (a type of sorbet with large ice crystals), layered with cream, served in individual wine glasses.

Serves 4

25 g (1 oz) sugar
75 ml (3 fl oz) water
250 ml (10 fl oz) passion fruit cordial or concentrated juice
20 ml (4 tsp) lemon juice
2 passion fruits, flesh removed
175 ml (7 fl oz) cream

To serve:
wafer biscuits

1. Dissolve the sugar in the water. Stir in the passion fruit cordial or juice, lemon juice and the passion fruit flesh. Freeze in a shallow container.
2. After 2 hours, beat the sorbet to break up the ice crystals, then return to the freezer for 1 hour. Beat again and return to the freezer for 1½ hours before beating for a third time. Finally, freeze for 1 hour by which time the sorbet should be fairly firm and ready to eat.
3. Place a scoop of sorbet in a tall stemmed wine glass, followed by a layer of cream. Repeat for another 3 or 4 layers and serve immediately with plain wafer biscuits.

FEUILLANTINE DE CITRON VERT

LANGDALE HOTEL
Great Langdale, Cumbria
Mr David Fairs with chef Philippe Batton
.

Thin, round sponge biscuits, filled with a rich lime mousse, served on a raspberry coulis.

Serves 6

For the feuillantine:
90 g (3½ oz) flour
65 g (2½ oz) caster sugar
65 g (2½ oz) butter, melted
2 egg whites
butter for greasing

For the mousse:
100 g (4 oz) caster sugar
4 egg yolks
juice and grated zest of 2 limes
90 g (3½ oz) butter, softened
125 ml (5 fl oz) double cream

For the sauce:
200 g (8 oz) raspberries
90 ml (6 tbsp) icing sugar, or to taste
10 ml (2 tsp) lime juice
10 ml (2 tsp) Cointreau or Kirsch (optional)

To serve:
fresh mint leaves
icing sugar
whole raspberries

1.   Preheat the oven to 220°C (425°F) mark 7.
2.   First prepare the feuillantine. Mix together the flour and sugar then stir in the melted butter and egg whites to form a batter.
3.   On greased baking sheets, spread the mixture to form 18 thin circles approximately 7.5 cm (3 inches) in diameter. It is easiest to drop a teaspoonful of mixture onto the baking sheet, then use the back of the spoon to spread to the required size and even thickness.
4.   Bake in the preheated oven for 2–3 minutes until cooked but without colour. Immediately lift the biscuits from the baking sheet, with a palette knife, and place flat on a wire rack to cool. Store in an airtight container until required.

5. Now prepare the lime mousse. In a bowl, cream the sugar and egg yolks together until pale and creamy. Add the lime juice. Transfer the mixture to a saucepan and heat, stirring with a balloon whisk, until the mixture boils. Pour the mixture back into a mixing bowl and continue to whisk for 2 minutes.

6. Cut the butter into small pieces and whisk, a knob at a time, into the mixture. Leave to cool.

7. Whip the cream and fold into the egg mixture with the grated lime zest. Cover and chill until set.

8. Prepare the raspberry sauce. In a liquidiser, process the raspberries, sugar and lime juice together until smooth, sieve.

9. Place a feuillantine wafer in the centre of a dinner plate, spread with a little lime mousse. Place another wafer on top, again spread with mousse and finally crown with a third wafer. Garnish the top with fresh mint leaves, dust with icing sugar and flood the base of the plate with raspberry sauce before serving.

BRAZILIAN BANANAS

THE REDFERN HOTEL
Cleobury Mortimer, Worcestershire

Mr & Mrs J. Redfern

.

Coffee and rum-soaked bananas topped with sweetened whipped cream.

Serves 4

30 ml (2 tbsp) lemon juice
5 large bananas, sliced
50 g (2 oz) dark brown sugar
50 g (2 oz) sultanas
90 ml (6 tbsp) strong black coffee (cold)
90 ml (6 tbsp) dark rum
375 ml (15 fl oz) double cream
15 ml (1 tbsp) caster sugar

1. Pour the lemon juice over the sliced bananas to prevent them discolouring.

2. Keeping a few slices for decoration, place the bananas in the base of a glass bowl. Sprinkle over the brown sugar, sultanas, coffee and rum.

3. Whip the cream with the caster sugar until it forms soft peaks then pipe or spoon over the bananas. Decorate with the remaining banana slices and chill until required.

APPLE & ORANGE FLAN

DEEPLEIGH FARM HOTEL
Langley Marsh, Somerset

Linda & Lester Featherstone

.

A creamy orange flan topped with apple strands, set in a rich shortcrust pastry case. Serve either hot or cold with cream.

Serves 10

For the pastry:
150 g (6 oz) butter
250 g (10 oz) flour
15 ml (1 tbsp) caster sugar
1 egg yolk
30–60 ml (2–4 tbsp) cold water

For the filling:
150 g (6 oz) butter
150 g (6 oz) caster sugar
8 egg yolks
75 g (3 oz) candied peel
grated zest of 1 orange
2 dessert apples

1. First prepare the pastry. Use fingertips to rub the butter into the flour until the mixture resembles fine breadcrumbs. Then stir in the sugar, egg yolk and enough of the water to bind into a firm dough. Cover and chill for 15 minutes.
2. On a lightly floured surface, roll out the pastry and use to line a deep-sided, 27.5 cm (11 inch) diameter, loose-bottomed flan ring. Chill for a further 5 minutes.
3. Preheat the oven to 170°C (325°F) mark 3.
4. Bake the pastry case blind for 15 minutes.
5. In a mixing bowl, beat together the butter, sugar and egg yolks until they are light and fluffy. Stir in the peel and orange zest.
6. Smooth the orange mixture over the pastry base. Core but do not peel the apples and grate over the top of the flan. Lightly pat down the grated apple. Bake in the preheated oven for 50 minutes or until golden and set.

DRUNKEN NUTTY FIGS

LONG'S RESTAURANT
Truro, Cornwall

Ian & Ann Long

.

Figs, marinated in port, stuffed with pecan nuts and served with clotted cream.

Serves 8

grated zest and juice of 2 oranges
90 ml (6 tbsp) honey
750 ml (1½ pints) port
1 kg (2 lb) dried figs
200 g (8 oz) pecan nuts
15–30 ml (1–2 tbsp) redcurrant jelly

To serve:
clotted cream

1. In a saucepan, mix together the orange zest, juice, honey and port. Heat until the honey has dissolved, then leave to cool.
2. Place the dried figs in a large mixing bowl and pour over the cooled port mixture. Cover and leave to soak overnight in a cool place.
3. Cut a small opening in each fig and carefully push a pecan nut into the centre. Press the edges of the fig together to enclose the nut stuffing.
4. Place the filled figs in a large saucepan and pour over the port marinade. Cover the pan and gently heat to poach the figs for 10 minutes.
5. Remove the figs from the pan and arrange in individual glass serving dishes, taking care that they look attractive through the glass sides.
6. Strain the port through a fine sieve over a clean saucepan, add the redcurrant jelly and heat, stirring until the jelly has dissolved. Increase the heat and boil until the liquid thickens slightly. Taste then leave to cool.
7. Ladle the cooled port over the figs, cover and refrigerate.
8. Remove the figs from the refrigerator 1 hour before serving, accompanied by a large bowl of clotted cream.

DATE & GINGER TOWERS WITH TOFFEE SAUCE

CHELWOOD HOUSE
Chelwood, Avon

Jill & Rudolf Birk with chef Michael Taylor

·

Individual date and ginger sponge puddings, covered in a hot toffee sauce, marbled with cream.

Serves 8

For the sponges:
butter for greasing
200 g (8 oz) butter, softened
50 g (2 oz) caster sugar
4 eggs
200 g (8 oz) self raising flour
5 ml (1 tsp) baking powder
150 g (6 oz) dates, chopped
150 g (6 oz) preserved stem ginger, chopped

For the sauce:
50 g (2 oz) butter
75 g (3 oz) soft brown sugar
65 g (2½ oz) demerara sugar
125 ml (5 fl oz) golden syrup
pinch of salt
200 ml (8 fl oz) double cream

To serve:
fresh dates
sprigs of mint

1. Preheat the oven to 220°C (425°F) mark 7.
2. Butter 8 tea cups, large ramekins or dariole moulds.
3. Cream together the butter and sugar until pale and light. Gradually add the eggs, then fold in the flour and baking powder. Stir in the dates and stem ginger.
4. Spoon the sponge mixture into the prepared moulds, only filling the moulds two thirds full. Stand the moulds in a roasting tin, filled with 2.5 cm (1 inch) of boiling water, cover with buttered greaseproof paper and place in the oven for 15 minutes until risen and firm.
5. Prepare the sauce by bringing all the ingredients, except the cream, to the boil together in a saucepan. Allow to bubble vigorously

for 5 minutes, then remove from the heat and, using a balloon whisk, whisk in half the cream.

6. Carefully turn the finished sponges out of the moulds, whip the remaining cream and spoon a mound of cream on top of each sponge. Pour the hot sauce over the cream topping, creating a marbled effect. Serve while warm, decorated with dates and mint.

SCOTCH CLOOTIE

ALTAMOUNT HOUSE HOTEL
Blairgowrie, Perthshire

Mr Ritchie Russell

A circular steamed pudding which should be served with whisky-flavoured cream.

Serves 4–6

125–150 g (4–5 oz) self raising flour
25 g (1 oz) raisins
25 g (1 oz) currants
25 g (1 oz) sultanas
65 g (2½ oz) shredded suet
40 g (1½ oz) caster sugar
15–25 g (½–1 oz) mixed spice
1 egg, lightly beaten
75 ml (3 fl oz) milk

To serve:
whipped cream flavoured with a tot of whisky

1. Mix together all the dry ingredients in a large bowl. Stir in the egg and enough of the milk to form a thick dough.
2. Line a 1.5 litre (3 pint) pudding basin with muslin. Fill the basin with the mixture, draw the muslin together around the pudding and tie tightly with string. Seal the basin securely with greaseproof paper or foil, so no water can touch the pudding during cooking.
3. Place a heatproof plate at the bottom of a large saucepan, stand the pudding basin on top and add water to come halfway up the side of the basin. Bring to the boil, cover and steam gently for 2½–3 hours, topping up the water as necessary.
4. Remove the basin from the saucepan and leave to stand for 10 minutes before taking off the string. Turn the pudding out onto a plate and serve with the whisky-flavoured cream.

STEAMED CHERRY & ALMOND SPONGE WITH BUTTERSCOTCH SAUCE

THE GRAPEVINE HOTEL
Stow-on-the-Wold, Gloucestershire
Mrs Sandra Elliott with chef Miss Lesley Pridmore

.

A light steamed sponge, flavoured with cherries and almonds, served with a sweet butterscotch sauce.

Serves 4

1 × 405 g (14.3 oz) can condensed milk
100 g (4 oz) butter
100 g (4 oz) caster sugar
2 eggs, lightly beaten
100 g (4 oz) self raising flour
50 g (2 oz) almonds, chopped
50 g (2 oz) glacé cherries, halved
2 drops almond essence
butter for greasing
500 ml (1 pint) single cream
50 g (2 oz) butter

1.   In a large saucepan, cover the unopened can of condensed milk with water and bring to the boil. Cook for 2 hours, checking the water level in the saucepan regularly – the tin will explode if the pan boils dry.
2.   Prepare the sponge by creaming together the butter and sugar until pale and creamy. Gradually beat in the eggs, then fold in the flour, nuts, cherries and almond essence.
3.   Lightly grease a 1 litre (2 pint) pudding basin. Pour the sponge mixture into the basin, cover tightly with greaseproof paper and secure with string. Steam in a saucepan of water for 1½ hours, topping up the water level regularly.
4.   In a saucepan, bring the cream to the boil, remove from the heat and whisk in the boiled condensed milk which should have the consistency of toffee. Whisk in the butter, a knob at a time, until the sauce is smooth and shiny.
5.   Carefully turn the steamed sponge out of the basin, pour the sauce over the top and serve.

DATE & APPLE TURNOVERS

TYGWYN GUEST HOUSE
Newquay, Cornwall

Mel, Clive & Mark Griffin

.

Puff pastry filled with a spicy date and apple mix. Serve hot or cold with plenty of cream or custard.

Serves 4–6

15 g (½ oz) butter
2 large cooking apples, peeled, cored and chopped
2.5 ml (½ tsp) grated lemon zest
5 ml (1 tsp) ground cinnamon
2 cloves
50 g (2 oz) caster sugar
30 ml (2 tbsp) dates, chopped
300 g (12 oz) puff pastry
1 egg, lightly beaten

To serve:
icing sugar to dust
whipped cream or custard

1.   Melt the butter in a saucepan and add the apples, lemon zest, cinnamon and cloves. Cover and cook over a low heat until the apples are soft. Remove the cloves and mash the apples to a smooth pulp. Add the sugar and dates then leave the turnover filling to go cold.
2.   Preheat the oven to 220°C (425°F) mark 7.
3.   On a lightly floured surface, roll out the puff pastry until 1.25 cm (½ inch) thick. Using a 7.5 cm (3 inch) round pastry cutter stamp out 6 circles in the pastry. Roll each pastry circle once again to halve its thickness, keeping the circle shape intact.
4.   Place a spoonful of apple mixture on one half of each piece of pastry. Brush the pastry edges with beaten egg, fold the pastry over to enclose the filling and press the edges together firmly to seal the pocket.
5.   Place the turnovers on a baking tray and refrigerate for 10 minutes. Brush the top of each turnover with beaten egg. Bake in the preheated oven for 15–20 minutes until the pastry has risen and turned golden.
6.   Using a palette knife or fish slice, remove the turnovers from the baking sheet and allow to cool slightly on a wire rack before dusting with sifted icing sugar and serving with cream or custard.

FRESH HERB FRITTERS WITH A LIGHT GINGER SAUCE

THE DENBIGH ARMS HOTEL
Lutterworth, Leicestershire
Mr & Mrs Eric Stephens

.

Fresh herbs and flowers coated in a sweet batter, fried until crisp and served on a hot, ginger cream sauce. If you cannot buy the suggested herbs and edible flowers listed in the ingredients for this recipe, try substituting other fresh herbs and flowers that are more easily available.

Serves 4

For the fritters:
100 g (4 oz) flour
pinch of salt
15 ml (1 tbsp) corn oil
125 ml (5 fl oz) water
1 egg white
16 sage leaves
16 large sprigs tarragon
15 large sprigs bush basil
4 sprigs bergamot
4 marigold flowers
25 g (1 oz) icing sugar

For the sauce:
250 ml (10 fl oz) double cream
30 ml (2 tbsp) ginger wine
15 g (½ oz) preserved stem ginger, finely sliced

1. Sift the flour and salt together into a bowl. Make a well in the centre and add the oil and water, beating until smooth. Leave to rest for 1 hour.
2. Whisk the egg white until stiff, then carefully fold into the batter mixture.
3. Wash and gently dry all the herbs, dust with icing sugar, place in the batter and leave to soak.
4. Heat clean oil in a deep fat fryer to 190°C (375°F).
5. Prepare the sauce. Heat the cream, ginger wine and sliced stem ginger together in a pan, bring to the boil and simmer until slightly thickened and shiny.

6. Using a slotted spoon or tongs, remove the herbs from the batter, shaking off excess batter as you lift. Plunge into the heated oil and cook until just golden. Drain thoroughly on kitchen paper and dust with icing sugar.

7. Coat the base of each plate with sauce and arrange several herb fritters on top. Serve immediately.

PLUM & RASPBERRY WALNUT CRUMBLE

DEEPLEIGH FARM HOTEL
Langley Marsh, Somerset

Linda & Lester Featherstone

·

A traditional crumble with a crunchy walnut topping. Serve with crème Anglaise (see page 205) or whipped cream.

Serves 8

1 kg (2 lb) plums, stoned
500 g (1 lb) raspberries
150 g (6 oz) granulated sugar (use more or less sugar depending on
the sweetness of the fruit)
350 g (14 oz) flour
150 g (6 oz) butter
150 g (6 oz) light brown sugar
250 g (10 oz) walnuts, chopped

To serve:
crème Anglaise (see page 205) or whipped cream

1. Preheat the oven to 200°C (400°F) mark 6.

2. Arrange the plums and raspberries over the base of a flat, ovenproof dish and sprinkle with the sugar.

3. Sift the flour into a bowl and lightly rub in the butter with fingertips, until the mixture resembles fine breadcrumbs. Stir in the brown sugar and walnuts.

4. Spoon the crumble mixture over the fruit and press down lightly. Bake in the preheated oven for 40–45 minutes until the top is light brown. Serve while hot with crème Anglaise or whipped cream.

APPLE & BLACKBERRY FUDGE CAKE

GALES
Llangollen, Clwyd
Richard & Gillie Gale

.

A hot upside-down sponge cake with a delicious fudge sauce.

Serves 6–8

For the fudge:
100 g (4 oz) butter
100 g (4 oz) soft brown sugar
100 g (4 oz) syrup
2.5 ml (½ tsp) vanilla essence

For the fruit topping:
500 g (1 lb) blackberries
500 g (1 lb) apples, cored and sliced

For the cake:
200 g (8 oz) soft brown sugar
200 g (8 oz) butter
200 g (8 oz) self raising flour
4 eggs
15 ml (1 tbsp) syrup
30 ml (2 tbsp) milk

To serve:
double cream

1. Preheat the oven to 150°C (300°F) mark 2.
2. First prepare the sauce. Place all the fudge ingredients together in a saucepan and boil gently until the butter has melted and the sugar dissolved.
3. Butter a 20 cm (8 inch) loose-bottomed cake tin and pour half the fudge sauce over the base. Spread the fruit over the fudge.
4. Put all the cake ingredients together in a mixer and process, adding a little more milk if necessary to form a smooth mix.
5. Spread the cake mixture over the fruit and bake in the hot oven for 30 minutes until the sponge is cooked, but not dry.
6. Carefully turn out onto a plate. Heat the remaining fudge sauce and spread over the top of the cake. Serve while hot with thick cream.

CHOCOLATE FLAPJACK PUDDING

HENLEY HOTEL
Bigbury-on-Sea, Devon

Mrs L. Beer

.

Mocca custard, crowned with a crunchy flapjack topping. Serve either hot or cold with cream. The ingredients for this dish are all standard store cupboard items so it's a wonderful 'whip together' pudding, that will really impress unexpected guests!

Serves 6

30 ml (2 tbsp) cornflour
250 ml (10 fl oz) milk
10 ml (2 tsp) instant coffee granules
45 ml (3 tbsp) drinking chocolate powder
250 ml (10 fl oz) water
30 ml (2 tbsp) caster sugar
150 g (6 oz) butter
300 g (12 oz) porridge oats
6 digestive biscuits, crushed
150 g (6 oz) light brown sugar

To serve:
double or clotted cream

1. Preheat the oven to 180°C (350°F) mark 4.
2. In a large bowl, mix the cornflour to a smooth paste with 30 ml (2 tbsp) of the milk.
3. Mix together the coffee powder, drinking chocolate, remaining milk and water in a saucepan. Heat, stirring, until the coffee and chocolate have dissolved. As soon as the mixture reaches boiling point pour onto the cornflour, stirring continuously with a balloon whisk. Pour the mixture back into the saucepan and add the caster sugar. Heat until the mixture has the consistency of a thick custard. Pour into a shallow ovenproof dish, or 6 large individual ramekins (there is as much depth of topping as custard so only half fill each container).
4. In a saucepan, melt the butter, then stir in the oats, biscuit crumbs and brown sugar until all the ingredients are evenly coated in butter. Sprinkle the flapjack mixture over the chocolate base and pat down lightly.
5. Bake in the preheated oven for 25–30 minutes until the top is lightly browned. Serve with cream.

CHRISTMAS BAKED APPLES

FROGGIES RESTAURANT
Knaphill, Surrey

Robin & Debbie de Winton

.

Meringue-topped baked apples, filled with brandy or rum-flavoured mincemeat.

Serves 4

butter for greasing
4 Bramley apples, washed and cored
3 eggs, separated
80 ml (16 tsp) good quality mincemeat
30 ml (2 tbsp) brandy or rum (optional)
grated zest and juice of ½ orange
100 g (4 oz) caster sugar
glacé cherries and angelica

To serve:
brandy custard or cream

1. Preheat the oven to 180°C (350°F) mark 4.
2. Butter a deep ovenproof dish.
3. Cut each apple in half horizontally and place in the prepared dish. Cover with buttered paper or lightly buttered foil and bake in the preheated oven for 30–40 minutes until just tender but not collapsing.
4. In a bowl, mix together the egg yolks, mincemeat, brandy or rum, orange zest and juice. Pile into the cooked apples, gently pressing down into the central cavity.
5. Turn the oven down to 150°C (300°F) mark 2.
6. Whisk the egg whites with 15 ml (1 tbsp) of the sugar until stiff, then gently fold in the remaining sugar. Pipe this meringue mixture over the apples, making sure the mincemeat filling is completely enclosed.
7. Sprinkle a little more caster sugar over the meringue and decorate with glacé cherries and angelica.
8. Return the apples to the oven for 15–25 minutes until the meringue topping is crisp and lightly browned all over. Serve while hot with brandy custard or cream.

BASIC STOCKS, SAUCES & TECHNIQUES

Today, many of us reach for a commercially produced cube when stock is listed as a recipe ingredient, so much so that many cooks have forgotten how to prepare their own stock at home. While cubes are an excellent, time-saving, convenience product, remember that they can have a strong, salty taste, which becomes unpleasant in sauces that are reduced, so concentrating the flavour. Many of the recipes in this book call for a 'good stock' and use of a home-produced fresh broth will greatly influence the flavour of the finished dish.

Stocks are relatively easy to prepare at home although they take time to make. Most stocks will keep for up to 3 days in the refrigerator, but it is probably better to use fish stock within 24 hours of preparation. If you have a freezer, batches of stock can be stored successfully for several months and, if freezer space is at a premium, stocks can be boiled and reduced before freezing in ice cube trays. Remember to dilute concentrated stock before use.

Generally, it is best to use a stock prepared from the same meat (fish, poultry or game) as that in the dish being cooked, but it isn't always essential. Just remember that a strong stock, say game, will mask the delicate taste of a light fish or chicken dish.

TO CLEAR A CLOUDY STOCK

1. Strain prepared stock into a saucepan and bring to the boil.
2. Add an egg white to the hot liquid and whisk with a balloon whisk until the stock froths. Remove the pan from the heat and leave to stand for several minutes.
3. Strain the stock through muslin or a jelly bag. Do not be tempted to push or hurry the liquid through the strainer, as this will cloud the liquid once more.

MEAT STOCK (BROWN STOCK)

For approximately 1.5 litres (3 pints)

750 g (1½ lb) meat bones (veal, beef or lamb), as much fat removed as
possible
2.5 ml (½ tsp) salt
2 carrots, chopped but not peeled
1 large onion, quartered (leave the skin on to give the stock colour)
2 sticks celery, chopped
4 peppercorns
either 1 bouquet garni
or 2 bay leaves and a selection of fresh herbs

1.   If you want a dark brown coloured stock, roast the bones in a hot
oven, 240°C (475°F) mark 9, for 45 minutes.
2.   Place all the ingredients in a large saucepan with 2.25–2.5 litres
(4½–5 pints) of water. Bring to the boil. Skim off any fat that collects on
the surface, cover and simmer for 2–3 hours.
3.   Strain, boil to reduce for a concentrated stock, or use as required.
4.   Chilled stock will collect a layer of fat on the surface; discard this
before use.

FISH STOCK

For approximately 1 litre (2 pints)

750 g (1½ lb) fish trimmings (head, bones, etc)
1.5 litres (3 pints) water
1 onion, chopped
1 carrot, chopped but not peeled
1 leek, chopped
1 stick celery, chopped
either 1 bouquet garni
or 2 bay leaves and a handful of fresh herbs
4 black peppercorns

1.   Wash the fish trimmings.
2.   Combine all the ingredients together in a large saucepan, bring to
the boil, cover and allow to simmer for 30 minutes, skimming from
time to time.
3.   Strain, boil to reduce for a concentrated stock or use as required.

FISH VELOUTÉ

This thickened fish stock is the basis of many traditional fish sauces.

For approximately 500 ml (1 pint)

25 g (1 oz) unsalted butter
25 g (1 oz) flour
500 ml (1 pint) good fish stock (see page 200)
seasoning

1. Melt the butter in a saucepan, stir in the flour to form a roux and cook for 2 minutes until it develops a sandy texture. Take care that the roux does not brown, or it will colour the sauce.
2. Lower the heat and gradually stir in the stock. Increase the heat and continue to cook until the sauce thickens to a smooth, creamy consistency, stirring constantly. Allow to simmer for 3 minutes, season and use as required.

POULTRY STOCK (WHITE STOCK)

For approximately 1 litre (2 pints)

3 cloves
1 small onion, peeled
500 g (1 lb) poultry carcasses, all skin and meat removed
1 carrot, chopped but not peeled
2 sticks celery, chopped
either 1 bouquet garni
or 2 fresh bay leaves and a handful of fresh herbs

1. Stick the cloves into the onion.
2. Place all the ingredients together in a large saucepan, cover with water and bring to the boil. Simmer for 1–1½ hours, skimming off the grey scum which forms on the top with a slotted spoon. Turn off the heat and leave the stock to cool in the pan for 1 hour, then strain to remove the carcasses and vegetables.
3. Boil to reduce for a concentrated stock, or use as required.

4. Chilled stock will collect a layer of fat on the surface; discard this before use.

Note: To prepare a brown poultry stock, roast the carcasses for 30 minutes, until coloured, before boiling.

COURT BOUILLON

A wine and vegetable stock which can be used for poaching fish or when steaming food to give added flavour to the finished dish.

For approximately 1.5 litres (3 pints)

1.5 litres (3 pints) water
250 ml (10 fl oz) white wine
250 g (10 oz) carrots, chopped
2 medium onions, sliced
2 sticks celery, sliced
either 1 bouquet garni
or 3 bay leaves and a bunch of fresh herbs
pinch of salt
4 black peppercorns

1. Place all the ingredients together in a large saucepan, bring to the boil and simmer for 30 minutes.
2. Leave the stock to infuse and cool. Strain and use as required.

TO SKIN A TOMATO

Either use the tip of a knife to make a small nick in the skin of each tomato and place in a mixing bowl. Pour boiling water over the tomatoes to cover, slowly count to 10, then drain. Plunge the tomatoes into ice cold water. It should then be relatively easy to peel the skin away.

Or spear a tomato with a knife or fork and hold over the naked flame on a gas hob. The skin will blacken and 'pop' as it loosens from the flesh. Rotate the tomato until all the skin is loosened, then peel away.

BROWN SAUCE

Use this sauce to thicken, give colour and add flavour to gravy and casseroles.

For 500 ml (1 pint)

25 g (1 oz) butter
1 carrot, chopped but not peeled
1 onion, quartered but not peeled
2 sticks celery, chopped
50 g (2 oz) streaky bacon, or bacon rind
25 g (1 oz) flour
750 ml (1½ pints) beef stock (see page 200)
bouquet garni
30 ml (2 tbsp) tomato purée
5 ml (1 tsp) Worcestershire Sauce
seasoning

1.   Melt the butter in a large saucepan and cook the vegetables and bacon for 10 minutes until browned.
2.   Stir in the flour and cook gently for 2 minutes. Gradually stir in the stock until the mixture has cooked through and thickened. Add the bouquet garni, tomato purée, Worcestershire Sauce and seasoning.
3.   Cover and simmer gently for 1 hour, stirring occasionally.
4.   Strain, taste and adjust seasoning, then use as required.

Note: If the sauce is to be stored for several hours before use, cover the top closely with clingfilm or lightly buttered greaseproof paper to prevent a skin forming.

KEY TO SUCCESSFUL ROUX-BASED SAUCE MAKING

*   Cook the roux (flour and butter paste) until it develops a sandy texture before adding any liquid.
*   Add slightly warmed, or room temperature, liquid to a roux.
*   Stir liquid gradually into a roux, making an even paste or sauce after each addition.
*   Stir sauces constantly during preparation.

SAVOY BISCUITS

For approximately 20 biscuits

butter for greasing
4 eggs, separated
150 g (6 oz) caster sugar
grated zest of 1 lemon
150 g (6 oz) flour, sifted

1. Preheat the oven to 180°C (350°F) mark 4. Thoroughly grease 2 baking sheets.
2. In a bowl, beat together the egg yolks, sugar and lemon zest until very pale and creamy.
3. In a separate bowl, whisk the egg whites until they form a soft froth.
4. Beat the flour into the egg yolk mixture followed by the egg whites, and continue whisking for several minutes.
5. Using a spoon, trail lines of the mixture over the prepared baking sheets to form long fingers and bake in the preheated oven for 5 minutes until cooked through but not coloured.
6. Cool on wire racks and store in an airtight container.

PRALINE

Ground nuts and caramel. Praline will keep for 6 months if stored in an airtight container and can be used as a flavouring for mousses and creams or sprinkled over the top of desserts for decoration.

For approximately 200 g (8 oz) praline

100 g (4 oz) granulated sugar
100 g (4 oz) mixed nuts (predominantly almonds)
oil for greasing

1. Put the sugar and nuts into a heavy-based saucepan and cook over a moderate heat, stirring constantly, until the sugar has caramelised and the nuts become shiny with sugar coating.
2. Quickly pour the mixture onto an oiled baking tray and leave until completely cool and set.
3. Break into manageable pieces and grind into a fine powder in a liquidiser or coffee grinder.

CRÈME ANGLAISE

A real vanilla custard that can be served with almost any dessert or gâteau.

For approximately 1 litre (2 pints)

either 1 vanilla pod, halved lengthwise
or 5 ml (1 tsp) vanilla essence
1 litre (2 pints) milk
pinch of salt
8–10 egg yolks
150 g (6 oz) caster sugar

1. If using a vanilla pod, scoop out the seeds from the centre.
2. Place the milk, vanilla (pod and seeds) and salt into a saucepan. Bring to the boil, remove from the heat and leave to infuse for 15 minutes.
3. Beat together the egg yolks and sugar until the mixture becomes pale.
4. Strain the milk, then gradually whisk into the egg mixture. Pour the resulting liquid back into the saucepan and heat gently for 10 minutes, stirring constantly.
5. As soon as the custard has thickened slightly, turn off the heat and leave the liquid to cool, stirring from time to time to prevent a skin forming.

Index